Conversations with Canadian Novelists Part One

Conversations with Canadian Novelists

Part One

Donald Cameron

Macmillan of Canada/Toronto

ISBN 0-7705-0942-8

Some sections of this book appeared previously in
Canadian Fiction, The Mysterious East, Quill and Quire,
and *Saturday Night.*

Printed in Canada

Contents

Foreword:

More than most books, this volume represents a sort of collaboration. The University of New Brunswick awarded me a Summer Research Grant to begin the project, and an early leave of absence in which to complete it. A research grant from the Canada Council paid for travel, transcription, tapes, typing, and various other expenses. Several publishers and libraries provided books and other materials which I used in preparing for the interviews. To all these institutions I am indebted.

Parts of the book have been broadcast by the Canadian Broadcasting Corporation, and others have been published in *Quill and Quire, Saturday Night, The Journal of Canadian Fiction*, and *The Mysterious East*. I am grateful for permission to use again material that first appeared in their pages. The published texts are selected and condensed; copies of the original tapes and the full transcripts are on deposit in the library of the University of New Brunswick.

One or two of the interviews were transcribed by Cheryl Dukeshire and Peggy Pitt, but Kini Savage devoted many weeks and a great deal of enthusiasm to the thankless task of transferring mumbles, gurgles, and laughter from tape to paper. Above all, the novelists themselves treated me with exceptional generosity. They went out of their way to see me, gave me as much time as I wanted, patiently corrected the final texts, permitted me to use the interviews as I saw fit, and in several cases entertained me in their homes and even fed me and put me up for the night. The book would have been impossible without their co-operation, of course, but never was co-operation more generously given. I hope they will enjoy the resulting book as much as I enjoyed gathering the material in it.

The successes of the book belong to all these people. But the failures belong to the organizer of the whole project — in other words, to me.

DONALD CAMERON

This book is dedicated to the people with whom it was created:

— to the novelists included in it, in gratitude for the pleasure they have given me both in their books and in person;

— to Margaret Laurence especially, whose candid and stimulating conversation over several years first suggested the possibilities of such a book as this;

— to Kini Savage, peerless secretary, assistant, friend, and cheering section.

Conversations
with
Canadian
Novelists
Part One

Ernest Buckler:

A Conversation with an Irritated Oyster

Ernest Buckler's shyness is legendary, and when I telephone him from Halifax he is friendly, but quite uncertain about whether or not he can sustain an interview. "Don't assume that because he says you can come, you're going to get an inter-

*view," caution my friends at the CBC in Halifax. They regale
me with yarns about Buckler hiding among the rows of corn
rather than face a buxom and very assertive lady interviewer
bristling with loaded questions and cameras.*

*My family and I drive up to Buckler's serene white farm-
house in Centrelia, just outside Bridgetown, only a few miles
from Dalhousie West, where he was born sixty years ago.
Buckler is not the tall, angular farmer some of his pictures
suggest; he is slight, almost frail, no more than medium
height. Though he is obviously shy, he makes us welcome,
introduces us to his second cousin up from the States, pours a
glass of Cinzano.*

*We talk for an hour or so, and then, eager and efficient, I
pull out my tape recorder. Buckler freezes, then remembers
that he too has a Uher tape recorder but isn't sure how to use
it. We go into his workroom to look at it. Buckler sits down in
the living room again, surrounded by cousin, interviewer,
interviewer's wife and baby, and freezes again. I turn the
tape off, and Buckler relaxes. "Look," I say, "let's turn it on
and go on chatting, and if nothing comes of it, what the hell."
Okay: and at that moment Ernest Buckler takes a deep breath,
gathers his thoughts, and launches into an exceptionally
articulate and entertaining conversation.*

CAMERON: What are the advantages and disadvantages, for a
writer, of living in the Maritimes?
BUCKLER: Well, of course, it all boils down to the problem of
isolation of the artist, doesn't it? if I can use so pretentious a
word. And I don't think that isolation is the problem, because
nobody in whatever he writes is ever writing about anything
but himself. And I think you can find yourself, can find what
you have to write about, much better in isolation than you
can if you are inside a clique. When too many writers get
together it gets to be a kind of masturbatory enterprise. They

tend to rub themselves off against each other, and they tend to talk too much. And once you've talked a thing out, you've had it.

CAMERON: You don't write it.

BUCKLER: No. No, you can't get back with the same impetus. You have to conserve your orgasm for the thing itself. Although again, in another way it's kind of a good thing to be with other writers, or other people of your same guild. You don't get the abject loneliness which is almost the *sine qua non* of the writer's art. But once your loneliness is alleviated you think, what the hell, I'll have a ball. Not that I classify myself in the same category as people who produce pearls or ambergris, but it is the *sick* whale that produces the ambergris, it is the *irritated* oyster which produces the pearl. So I think if you are entirely happy in the company of your compatriots, and all this, you're just simply having too good a time to be bothered sitting on your bloody bottom and straining or on occasion retching for words which will mean something.

CAMERON: Did you always want to be a writer?

BUCKLER: I had no burning desire to write. Well, of course, everybody writes, and in my juvenile phase I did indeed write all these short stories, these very *avant-garde* short stories where nobody has a name, where everybody is called just "he" or "she" — and being very young you write these burning poems about death, you know. I think I outlived that phase rather quickly. It's a phase that every young writer goes through. You write about death when death is not near; it's hard to write about death when death is near.

So it was just a fluke; as it happens, my sister and her husband were coming home from Montreal and they picked up this magazine, *Coronet*, which used to be a first-class magazine. There was a contest in it, so I thought, "What the hell, I'll try it" — and I got the first prize. After that I got into *Esquire*, which was an allied publication. And then I got into the writing bit.

CAMERON: Almost by accident.

BUCKLER: Entirely by accident, and I think everything I write is by accident. No, no, I'm kidding you really. It's not entirely by accident. There *are* days when you think it's just on the tip of your tongue to be Shakespeare. You sit and sweat a while—it's almost like constipation, really; it's like going to the john at a certain time every day. You'll eventually have a movement. This is the way you do it. don't sit and wait for inspiration. Because inspiration is a fallacy. Inspiration is only the little click that you feel after you've put in all the sweat and tried to wipe all the sweat out. And the inspiration is when you think, "Bang! I've got it." But it's because of all the work you have put into it before, groping, groping, here and there and here and there—suddenly this back work has come to a head, like a boil.

CAMERON: You have a very regular pattern of work, then?

BUCKLER: Yes, I can't work in the morning at all because, as I said to you, I think mornings should be prohibited by law. I cannot collect two sentences, I can't put a subject to a predicate in the morning. In the afternoon I'm reasonably articulate. But I'm sort of a night man. In the evening if there is anything to blossom, it does blossom, and this is the time when you get your mower out, and you mow it down, and you reap it, and you bundle it.

CAMERON: A pattern like this ought to work in a rural area where your neighbours have farm work to do. You don't have a lot of nighthawks around.

BUCKLER: Well, of course, this is difficult in the country, too. You know, you are inclined to feel that if you live in the country your time is absolutely your own. By golly, it is *not*. Of course my time when I write has to be absolutely my own. If there are a bunch of blackbirds caucusing in the lilac bush outside the window they disrupt me. I have to have absolute silence, absolute quiet. And in the country this is just precisely the time when somebody will come in, some gal, you know, who'll talk for hours on end as to whether her husband prefers turnips in the stew or cauliflower. You don't want to offend them — because I love them dearly and they are the source of whatever talent or substance I have in my writing. But mind you, it's most distracting.

On the other hand, I think that if you don't have other things on your mind you can't write. You sit down, it's an absolutely clear day, and you think, Now, it's going to come today — and all you get is this blank white sheet, and the blank white sheet is the blank white sheet of the day really. So I've always found that when I was actively farming — you know, had cows to worry about, whether it was their time to be taken to the bull, or whether the peas were lolling in the rows and should be propped up — this I thought at the moment a distraction, but actually I think you write best when you're getting this kind of influx to your consciousness. When your consciousness seems to be a *tabula rasa* and you can write on it when you indeed want to write, paradoxically you find that you're stymied.

CAMERON: Do you miss the kind of stimulation you get from, say, live theatre, or art galleries or symphonies?

BUCKLER: Well, art is a blind spot of mine, music is a blind spot of mine — I'm afraid (to make a terrible confession) that I like *Aida*. And of course you can get *Aida*, you can get *Aida* with Leontyne Price. You can get her on recordings. You can get Gielgud. You can get almost everybody in better form than when they are performing on stage. As for books, well, we have this almost miraculous thing, this bookmobile. I simply couldn't live without this thing. When they first came around I thought it would have sort of dreary things like *How to Stuff a Duck* — but my God, you can get anything from Aeschylus to Mailer. I have books, correspondence, I have theatre by gramophone, so I don't feel bereft in that sense — although there is, undeniably, the extra subsistence you get from the actual performance of things — and I do miss *that*.

CAMERON: And you'd rather read a writer's works than talk to him.

BUCKLER: Writers, by and large, are the dreariest people you can possibly know, because they are just stuffed with words, like dry-bread dressing up a Christmas Eve goose's ass. You can't subsist on writers alone; I mean you subsist on people who really live, who are not looking at what they are doing all the time. A writer is always schizophrenic—I am myself. You have to be acting to get some substance; you also, at the same time, have to be a spectator, you have to observe people who just act simply, and are not introspective in the least, and draw your conclusions from them. And this is what you *don't* get when you associate almost entirely with writers. Because they are just word-guys.

CAMERON: Is this another advantage of living in a small town, where you get to know various people fairly well?

BUCKLER: This is what I was trying to bring out in *Ox Bells and Fireflies*. You don't have to wander all over the bloody world and explore every niche and cranny in it to find out how people behave. In a small community like this even, you have a representation of every kind of action, of every kind of psychological mode. The whole thing, the whole macrocosm, is here in microcosm. You don't have to know any more people than these to know what is going on in the human psyche. So this is why I haven't felt the exorbitant need to travel; I feel it's pretty well all here.

CAMERON: Do you feel a special richness of character here, that's especially pronounced in the Maritimes?

BUCKLER: Of course it is. Yes, I think in the Nova Scotia country, almost specifically in the country where I live, you get the universals more than you do almost anywhere else. I've found this a great sustenance. It is probably because one is always writing about one's background and of course one is always writing about oneself, as I've said before, but I think you do get every psychological—a word I hate—facet and ambiance—another word I hate—more here than probably anywhere. You don't need to budge from here to get the whole story.

CAMERON: Do local people see themselves in the characters of your novels?

BUCKLER: When the first book came out, I had an awful time around here, because all kinds of people were identifying themselves with this or that person in the book and there was a great clamour. Although strangely enough the people were identifying themselves with people who were not the people I had written about. But fact is no good novelistically. Of course, *Ox Bells and Fireflies* is, as I call it, a "fictive memoir", and it's basically fact. But when I think that fiction probably can construe the circumstances better than fact baldly states, I do embroider, I do change, and I don't really think this is trickery. Because fiction is so often not only more emphatic, but it's *truer* than fact. If you don't have facts to start with, you don't get anywhere. But when you start with a fact, I think you can transfigure it by embellishment, or twists, or perspective of one kind or another, which is much truer eventually than the thing as it actually happened.

CAMERON: Life doesn't take the shape of art.

BUCKLER: No, I don't think life imitates art. I don't think art imitates, delineates life, not precisely. There is a difference between photography and painting, I guess. Not that I'm a master at it, but I certainly know how I think it should go. You can't photograph, because this is just dull. I think you have to paint; I think the writer has to paint life.

CAMERON: You have pretty exacting standards.

BUCKLER: Well, you build up the thing in your mind, you know — you worry and fret and sweat, all this when perhaps it couldn't matter less. And I'm inclined to think that it doesn't matter one goddam bit in the world. But of course when you're starting, and when you're writing, you have to *believe* in your *guts* that this *does* matter, what you're trying to say and what you're going to say. But when you get to the point, when you think, Well hell, if I were *damn near* Shakespeare it wouldn't matter one flick of the dice, then you're in a bad bind.

CAMERON: I'd rather you were Buckler. One Shakespeare's enough.

BUCKLER: Yes, but the son of a bitch, he *said* everything! It's Elizabethan England, never mind. He says things which are so universal! So what is some half-assed kook, like myself, trying to do, to write? And of course there are only about five things to write about, and all you can do is change the locale, and with a little bit of particular embellishment make it sound or look like a different story, but it's the same old crazy human story. And Shakespeare has said it consummately, Dante has said it consummately— so what are *you* going to do? It's too late to be a bricklayer, it's too late to be almost anything. You have had this kind of illusion that you can say something differently, say something more emphatically, say something more piercingly, than anybody has said before, and this is the only thing you can operate on, when you start to write. But by God, when it gets later on and you start to think too much: is it any good? and you decide it is not bloody well Shakespeare or Dante, what do you do?

CAMERON: Can you, yourself, judge? Isn't this something you get as feedback, from people who have read the books?

BUCKLER: This is the only reward you have—never mind the royalties, which are not much. When *The Mountain and the Valley* came out I used to get letters saying, "This thing has meant a great deal to me," and of course that is the only kind of reward that you have. I think the nicest letter —well, the most amusing one—I ever had was from somebody in Cape Breton. Talk about succinctness: he wrote me, and he said, "I enjoyed your book very much. It was such clear print. Sincerely." You know the crazy letters you get. One gal in Seattle, Washington, gave all her measurements. She said, Ernest Redmond Buckler, your very name thrills me. I can just see you on a white charger rescuing—she did indeed say this—damsels in distress. My God, myself on a white charger! I'm scared shitless of horses. One kicked me in the head at thirteen.

CAMERON: What a marvellous letter.

BUCKLER: And I received some really fine letters from others whom the book had apparently hit kind of hard. But I'm so surprised at this, because—my golly, this is such an old-fashioned novel. It kind of celebrates families being together; it celebrates, if you don't mind the expression, love. If love could be had in a cube like LSD, I think all the kids would be going for it like wild. It's the most extraordinary thing.

If you think of a God up there—well, I'm not too hot on God—but if you think of God, how incredible that he could have made up a thing like love, which I think is the only answer to anything. I'm not quite a flower-guy—but my golly, if you have love you don't care about much else, do you? All this worrisome thing, the way the world is going on, if you have love you can shake it off. You have to give it to God for having thought it up. Again, for having thought up humour. If you were sitting down to make a world how on earth would you have thought up humour? I mean not only humour in the big sense, but somebody's turning up at the Ladies' Aid in a funny hat and all the other gals laugh at it. Can you possibly conceive of God at the bottom of this? If indeed he *is* at the bottom of it, he's not a bad guy.

CAMERON: Do you get called sentimental?

BUCKLER: There's a very, very thin line between sentiment and sentimentality, and I think that *sentiment* is just fine. I think this thing about hardening against sentiment is what kills people. Of course sentimentality, *blatant* sentimentality, is a different thing altogether. But I think the only thing in this world that saves us at all is *feeling*, and it seems to me you bloody well go the hell ahead and *feel*. And never mind what people say. I think heart is a big word, because it has the same letters as earth, as I've said somewhere. Heart is what we live by; I don't think we live by mind, I think we live by heart. And I like people with heart. I'm sure you have heart.

CAMERON: I'm glad you think so!

September 1, 1968

Ernest Buckler:
Biography and Bibliography

Ernest Buckler was born in Dalhousie West, Nova Scotia, in 1908. He graduated from Dalhousie University in 1929, working summers at a resort in Connecticut, and in 1930 received the M.A. in philosophy from the University of Toronto. He worked for five years with a Toronto insurance company, but returned to Nova Scotia in 1936. Since then he has lived near Bridgetown, combining farming and writing; in recent years he has devoted himself completely to writing. In 1957 and 1958 he won the President's Medal of the University of Western Ontario for the best Canadian short story of the year. He holds honorary doctorates from the University of New Brunswick and from Dalhousie University.

Fiction

The Mountain and the Valley (1952)
The Cruellest Month (1963)
Ox Bells and Fireflies (1968)

Criticism

Gregory Cook, ed., On Ernest Buckler *(1972)*

Roch Carrier :

You Have To Take
Some Risk To Tell the Truth

*Over beer and a sandwich in a small tavern near Place des Arts,
Roch Carrier is telling me it is exciting to be a writer in Québec.
His voice is extraordinarily soft, at times little more than a*

whisper; he wears a sports jacket and slacks, with a light orange shirt that adds just a touch of modishness; his straight dark hair is by current standards short and conservatively cut.

But it is hard later to remember these things, for what lingers is Carrier's intensity, the way his compact, short body leans into the conversation, the glint in his eyes, the vibrancy of his voice. He finds it difficult to speak for long periods in English, and he apologizes for his inadequate grasp of my language. It takes courage for him to be interviewed in English, I realize, but he thinks the interview project is important; he is happy to do what he can to help. We are building the literature of our country (or countries), and he believes in a constant interchange between readers, writers, and critics. He is a very warm, approachable man, and within minutes we seem to know one another well. I feel a good interview, a memorable encounter, coming on.

After lunch we sink into deep armchairs in one of Place des Arts's plush foyers. Carrier's slow explanations and sibilant yeses hang in the air. And for me, at least, a memorable encounter does occur.

CAMERON: Your novels are often terrifying and frightening, but they're also very funny. They're like folk tales, in a way.
CARRIER: Yes, because the comedy in my novels does not come from reading, or from literary tradition: it comes from something which was lived. In my family or in my village, people there have a kind of sense of seeing things and people more big and more funny and more brave than they are. It's in that living tradition that I learned to build up a character, to build up an action, and not in a literary way. A novel like *La Guerre, Yes Sir!* is not a novel which takes place in a tradition, because to write that novel I really had to forget everything I had learned in books and in La Sorbonne, everything. I tried to find in myself everything in that book. Everything which was in

myself was from my village, from people I know. Tha
it's very difficult to situate that novel in a literary tradi.
tried to find something which was instinctive.

CAMERON: But the village in the book is not exactly St. Ju
de Dorchester. How did you build that village in the book o
of the village in south Québec?

CARRIER: That book was not made the way people think.
When I came back from Europe in '64, after five years away,
the *révolution tranquille* was just taking place in Québec; people
were concerned about new political problems. The change was
almost unbelievable for someone who was not in Québec. I
met friends on my return: many of them were separatists, and I
could not understand what was happening. I told myself that
maybe by writing I could really live what people had lived
before, some years before. I thought that taking a little village,
which is a microcosm, would be a good place for me to let live
all those forces which were in the French Canadian. I did not
want to understand the situation in an intellectual way, because
when you are intellectual you always go in a system, and I did
not want to have any system. So I told myself, if I can let free
those forces in a French Canadian, I will look at what will
happen. Believing that, I began to write *La Guerre*.

CAMERON: Did you feel at the end of it that you did understand a lot more than you had?

CARRIER: Yes, I think so, I think so. When the book was published, many people in Québec thought it's a novel of old times,
but I heard also it's a prophetic novel. During the October
events, I heard, many times: You prophet!

CAMERON: Did the novel change you yourself? Do you feel
differently about being Québécois?

CARRIER: When *La Guerre* was finished, I had the deep feeling
that I had to continue to try to understand, and I found that if
the events of *La Guerre* were happening like they happened
in *La Guerre*, there were other causes. That's why I wrote
Floralie, to understand what was in a French Canadian other
than a political feeling, other than that aggressiveness against

n Canada. The book *Floralie* is about Catholic consci-
I think that Catholic conscience has a great influence on
way we live now, on the way we look at problems and try
give them solutions. Many people became involved in
olitics in the same way that they were involved in religion some
years ago, with the same severeness, the same aggressiveness.

CAMERON: Catholicism also seems to have left a very rich folk
imagination that you explore in *Floralie*.

CARRIER: It's not imaginative: I think everything is real. It's
a realistic novel. What a young French-Canadian girl thinks
about in the night, that's what I tell in the novel.

CAMERON: Yes, but it's internal reality. Presumably even in
Québec you didn't have Néron chugging through the woods
with his car full of children.

CARRIER: Yes, yes, why not? I thought of it, so it's true.

CAMERON: Well, *I* won't argue. What sort of thing are you
doing now?

CARRIER: I don't know where I'm going exactly. I am working
now on another novel. It's quite different from what I've
written, but it's quite similar at the same time. I am not a formal
writer, I don't really experiment with form. Why, I don't
know. In France now there are a lot of very interesting formal
experiments in the novel, but all those experiments were done
against a tradition, and here in Québec we have no tradition of
novels. So I told myself, let's write things as I see them, the most
efficient way; and after that we'll build novels, if we have time,
which are beautiful in form. It's not very high as a philosophy,
but I think we have to clear the way. After that our children
will do another thing. I write something, and I look at it, and
I say, No, ça marche pas, it's no good. Then I try something
else — that's the way I write.

CAMERON: You've tried a lot of things, in your short stories
especially.

CARRIER: When I wrote the short stories in *Jolis Deuils*, like
those translated in *Ellipse*, I was in France and I was very poor,
but it was the free life and among all my reading I had a little

time to write. So I used to write two or three short s
day, because I was discovering the world. Everything w.
for me, just everything in Europe. I saw a statue with a p
on his head, and it was a subject of a short story. I had a
of sensibility that made me able to feel something deep
everything. Reality was like a wall, and I had to find somethir
on the other side of the wall. I remember one day it was very
cold in my apartment and I wrote a short story, which is the
first in *Ellipse*, about that winter in which everybody's cold,
all the city is frozen. I had to go on the other side of the mirror,
if you want. Why, I don't know — but it was a kind of venture
to go, d'aller plus loin, si vous voulez, to go further. And those
characteristics suit my way of feeling things very well. We
can find them in my novels. In *Floralie* or in *La Guerre*, or *Il
Est Par Là, Le Soleil*, the third novel, we had something of
those short stories. I need to go a little bit further than the
reality.

CAMERON: Could you do a whole novel just dealing with the
behind-the-mirror thing that you get in the short stories?

CARRIER: I think I will succeed in doing that. You see, I am
learning everything: I am learning life, I am learning a way of
writing. Far, very far, I see a kind of big book in which everything I learn will be found, and every novel, every short story
I write, prepares me to do that kind of book. In that book there
will be formal experiments, but it will be a great disorder, if
you want, like life. I will be myself in the book, and it will be
interesting to be in, but I have so much to learn — !

CAMERON: Do you feel very young at the moment?

CARRIER: Yes.

CAMERON: Is that new, or were you always like that?

CARRIER: I was always the same. I never feel old, I never feel
really tired, except maybe intellectually. But it's not tiredness
in approaching life. Everything is great, everything is to be
discovered, every person is to be more known. Yes, I think I
feel young, and I feel young because I know the very tiny
importance of one man. I read the papers and I see friends who

۱ the biggest one, the greatest one. It's funny but it's
y serious for me, because a man is always learning, he's
s trying to understand better, and that's my kind of in-
ement.

ᴍᴇʀᴏɴ: Is that why you left teaching to become a drama-
rge?

ᴀʀʀɪᴇʀ: Yes, I left university to live the adventure of the
theatre, and it's great, I am learning a lot. Maybe in two or
three years it will be too small, and I will have to find something
else.

ᴄᴀᴍᴇʀᴏɴ: The first work you ever did for the theatre was the
adaptation of *La Guerre*, wasn't it?

ᴄᴀʀʀɪᴇʀ: Yes. One day, it was a spring day, I had a phone call
asking me if I wanted to write an adaptation for the theatre
from my novel *La Guerre, Yes Sir!* and without thinking I
said Yes. And I did it. I had a big chance, and it was a good
success in Montréal. After that the Théâtre du Nouveau Monde
needed a play to go on a European tour; they asked for my
play and I said Yes. Everything went well in Europe, too. The
play was done in Paris and in Rennes. In Belgium we did
the play in five or six towns, including Brussels. In Switzerland
we played in Lausanne; in Luxembourg, we played in Luxembourg, and in Czechoslovakia we played in Prague and two
other cities.

ᴄᴀᴍᴇʀᴏɴ: How did the European audiences react to it? Did
they find it strange and exotic?

ᴄᴀʀʀɪᴇʀ: I was invited as a writer by the Canada Council to
do the tour, to learn about different audiences. I made two
main discoveries. First, the French my people spoke, which is
not *joual* but is Québécois dialect, could be understood everywhere in France and Switzerland. The most important discovery was that the only way of being international is to be
very national. The main theme of my play is the reaction of a
minority in front of a majority, and when we were in France
they understood very well. When we were in Switzerland
people there understood very well; they saw themselves in

front of the Germans. When we were in Brussels it was the same thing, the French people there feel as a minority in front of the Flamands. In Prague the Czechoslovakians feel as a minority in front of the Russians and in every review that was mentioned: that the play was Québécois, but it was also Belgian, or Swiss, or Czechoslovakian.

CAMERON: That must give you a tremendous feeling of confidence.

CARRIER: I am really not confident. It's a marvellous experience, that success, but it doesn't make me self-confident. On the contrary, I was unable to write for the theatre afterwards. The Théâtre du Nouveau Monde asked me to write a play, but I was really unable during the winter to write it, and I worked on a novel instead of writing a play. I lived that adventure, the theatre, for a year very deeply, and it's really too much for a man to feel. I had to sit down and to think of another thing, to forget about that, because when I was at my work table, within myself I was preparing another *La Guerre*. If such a play worked one time, if it was efficient one time, instinctively you want to repeat it. That's very very very bad. So this year I have to forget about that.

CAMERON: When you came to work in the theatre, did you find it difficult really to think as a dramatist rather than a fiction writer?

CARRIER: It was not very hard, but there were many problems. When you write a novel the way I write them, you're God. You create the temperature, you create the space, you can do everything. On the stage you have to accept some limits. Look at the stage here; it's ninety feet wide. In my novel *La Guerre*, I had some dialogue between Bérubé and Molly in bed, and when I wrote the adaptation I automatically saw a bed on the stage. But let's try to put the bed on a ninety-foot-wide stage. That makes no sense at all, so I had to change that. And it's true you can be helped by the lights and the music, but everything, I think, is in the dialogue. The dialogue has to be very strong, much stronger than normal, to reach people. One has to find what is the most theatrical. The play *La Guerre* was not really theatrical, I must say, because it was a novel done on the stage. I could answer you better in some months, because when I am ready I will write something, a real creation written directly for the stage.

CAMERON: I was going to ask if that wouldn't be what you'd want to do now.

CARRIER: Yeah. It was good to have the security of a novel behind me, but I think that a man who writes for the theatre has to write for the theatre, to find a theatrical way. And at Théâtre du Nouveau Monde we are looking for a popular public, we have to find a popular way to be understood by that public. That's very difficult.

CAMERON: What kind of an audience did you get for *La Guerre*? Mostly middle-class people, or did you get some working people?

CARRIER: We noticed from the inquiries that a lot of people who did not usually come to the theatre came for *La Guerre*. I was very glad of that, but there was a kind of misunderstanding: they were coming to see a funny play about a wake.

CAMERON: And did they enjoy it?

CARRIER: Oh yes, yes. Somebody kept the time, and we had forty-five minutes of laughing during the play, so they laughed a lot. But there was a misunderstanding. The director, Albert Millaire, and I thought it was a tragedy. Both of us were in the back, watching the first words and the first reactions, and two seconds after the beginning there was a big laugh. We were almost crying, because of the misunderstanding there. I don't complain about it, though. It's better that the people come here even through a misunderstanding.

CAMERON: When you say *La Guerre* was intended to be a tragedy, do you feel the same way about the novel?

CARRIER: Yes.

CAMERON: Can you tell me why?

CARRIER: It's very sad for me. Every character is sad because he's condemned to failure. The only people who do not fail are père et mère Corriveau. They are simple; I think that they love themselves, and they are the only ones that are not failing their lives. But Philibert will fail, Bérubé will fail, Molly is failing—everybody is failing, and everybody maybe had many possibilities. They were reasonably intelligent, but life did not give them the opportunity of exploiting that intelligence, that force they had, so everybody is really condemned to be nothing and to live nothing. That's sad. Another thing which is sad is that inevitable war between the French and the English. For me it's really a conviction, that, which I found in writing my novel, that it was impossible not to collide. In the novel, I put all those contrary forces and I let them free, and ils se sont frappés.

CAMERON: You think that will happen in reality.

CARRIER: Yes, it will come. When I hear the news from Ireland, it's so near Québec. We will have another October event, maybe in December this time, and the army will come back, and there will be little smashes, but—

CAMERON: —eventually you see a big smash?

CARRIER: Yes. Let's say, in a cold way, you don't accept that somebody takes what's yours. I think that for an English Canadian Québec is his property. Ontario is not the property of a Québécois but I think that Ontarians feel that Québec is their property because it's part of the country, and nobody wants to lose what belongs to him. Québec will leave Confederation under new legislation maybe, but it's not possible to imagine Québec leaving smoothly. That's what I discovered by writing that book too: the villagers have nothing against the soldiers, the soldiers have nothing against the villagers, they are doing their job. But things go on, and the machine is running. They have to smash. I don't want that smash, and I remember a sentence by Richler one year ago in a magazine: he was saying that Québec was going through the same sterility as Ireland. And I was quite surprised to read what I was thinking myself. I don't want that sterility, I don't want that smash. So I decided to work, to do something in Québec, to continue to participate in the building of a literature, participate more and more in what I know, the cultural life, and maybe to try to have friends outside the frontier. I try to know a little bit more what's happening there. Maybe it will be possible to have a kind of collaboration. Naturally I prefer to try to find something we have in common; that's better than an opposition. So that's what I'm working on. The Québécois is very much frustrated because he doesn't feel he has his real part in Canada. I think we have to go outside, we have to take part.

CAMERON:　Something like touring the country with the English version of *La Guerre* might be tremendously useful.

CARRIER:　I think it would be, because the first task we have is to tell the truth. You have to take some risk to tell the truth.

CAMERON:　Is that how you see the writer's job? To tell the truth?

CARRIER:　It's the most honourable one, the most honourable task, I think. If we were a free country, and a rich country, if everybody around the world were well-nourished, writers could write perfect and formal novels, but instead we have to work in the street, in the garden. I think to tell the truth is the best way to live now.

CAMERON:　I think everybody, in any kind of work, asks himself these days, Is this the most useful thing to be doing now?

CARRIER:　Two years ago I was asking myself that question, and I had an answer. I thought it was important to give a lecture on Malraux, it was important to give a lecture on Corneille; it was *really* important, and I was trusting myself saying that. But at a certain time I was unable to trust myself, and I thought, It's time now to get out. I was speaking about telling the truth: my third novel, the sequel of *La Guerre*, tells the story of a young Québécois trying to live in Montréal. It's not an experience I lived myself, exactly, because I was much better prepared than my character, but it was the story of many many many Québécois who come to Montréal. The work here was English, and they were French paysans; the work here was technical, and they were badly prepared for it. It was a drama for them which has an influence on what is happening now. I did not live that experience but I think as a writer I had the task — le devoir, the duty — to speak in place of those who don't know how to speak. This experience has to be told. It's important that we know our past; it helps us to understand the present.

CAMERON: How do you manage to see things from the point of view of, say, Floralie? She's a woman thirty or forty years your senior, living in a village, an unquestioning Catholic and so on.

CARRIER: I don't know, exactly. I think I take myself as I am and I go in the reverse direction from what I live; and following that reverse logic, I can reach a woman like Floralie. Because without the chances I had, I could have been a man like Floralie. I don't know how these things happen, though; it's a mysterious chemistry. Flaubert described the work of a writer. He kept his diary about Madame Bovary and in one page he wrote, Today I was a horse, I was a leaf in autumn, I was a man, I was a woman, I was a lover. A writer is everything and everybody. At least he tries to be.

CAMERON: When it's really going well and you're working on a novel like *Floralie*, do you forget Roch Carrier?

CARRIER: Yes. There is a horse in the novel, and I became a horse. One day I was in St. Tropez and I was writing a short story about hockey. I was in my house and I was walking like this — and my wife asked, What are you doing? I said, I'm playing hockey — and it was true. I said that without thinking I was writing, but just trying to keep the feeling in my wrists.

CAMERON: Does the work stay with you all the time, or can you just throw it off when you go out to teach or work at the theatre?

CARRIER: I think of what I'm writing all the time — too much, I'm very preoccupied. But to write I sit down at my table. It's difficult to begin to put something on the paper, but after several minutes I become, like *hot*. And there, it's true, I *am* my character. It continues like that maybe for fifteen minutes at the most, and I am really what I have to be. After that there is a phone call or something, I don't know. I think I am very tired. Afterwards I continue to write, but not very long. But in the intense moment, I can write very very speedily. I spend one hour a day at my worktable, not more than that. But *every* day, *every* day.

CAMERON: At a special time?

CARRIER: No, when I am free. It's not very long, but if I write one hour a day I can do a lot of writing during a year.

CAMERON: How long does it take you to do a novel?

CARRIER: *La Guerre* was written very fast. It took me twelve days.

CAMERON: Twelve *days?*

CARRIER: Yes. It was very intense. For many many years I had thought about something like *La Guerre*, so I was ready for it; it was not new material. *Floralie* is more well-written than *La Guerre*, more formal, and it took me almost one year to write this book. The third one, *Il Est Par Là, Le Soleil*, took me a whole year.

CAMERON: How would a character like old Corriveau come to you?

CARRIER: Corriveau is the type of the old French-Canadian man, a strong man, married to weak little Floralie. Floralie was very much Catholic, so they made love by the hole in the night jacket; Father Corriveau was strong, and would like a woman, would like to drink, but Floralie was always there saying No, no, you have to be a good Catholic. So Father Corriveau is very frustrated, and at the wake we see his frustration, but at the same time the chance he took to liberate himself. He's the type of the old French-Canadian paysan. But I am Father Corriveau every time my wife finds I come home too late at night. It's something a man feels every day, not to be able to do what he wants to do, to fail.

CAMERON: How did you get into the third novel?

CARRIER: When *La Guerre* was finished, I had the feeling I had to go before that to understand other causes of the problem, so I wrote *Floralie*. But when *Floralie* was finished, everything was not told; I had to go after *La Guerre*, to see what would happen to young Philibert, the child who left the village at the end of *La Guerre*. Those three books were one book, finally. The novel I am now writing is different. The place is Montréal, and it will be a novel of the city. For many years I have wanted to tell the story of a building—the main character of my novel is a building. How that came about I don't know. Things come and they take importance, and I have to fight with them.

CAMERON: Are you following the life of the building itself?

CARRIER: I would prefer not to speak about what is not exactly finished. The building will be built, but it is a story of people involved in that building.

CAMERON: Many novelists say that when they're working on a novel they can't discuss it. Do you feel the same way about it?

CARRIER: Yes and no. I think I could speak about what is written now and what I intend to do, but I want to preserve a kind of freedom, you see. If I say to somebody, This thing will happen, instinctively I will have the feeling that I should write what I said, or do the contrary of what I said. When we write we have choices to make. I think the choice of something, the choice of a road, the choice of a word, the choice of an action, must come when the pencil is on the paper, at that point when everything is hot.

CAMERON: In that big book you see far off, you told me you would really be yourself. Do you feel you haven't been, so far?

CARRIER: No, not exactly. When I read the proofs of *La Guerre* I was almost shocked, because that book was so different from what I am and what I was. It was something strange, mysterious. And the same for *Floralie*, and the same for Philibert. Those books permitted me to discover a part of myself which was unknown to me. When I say those books are strangers, they are not really strangers, because it is impossible for a writer to invent what is actually unknown to him. I had not lived directly those things, but I had had repercussions on me of those lives lived by other people. It's so difficult for me to try to be intelligent in English, and it's also difficult because all the things we are speaking about are difficult even in French. I explain things very badly.

CAMERON: No, you make more sense in your second language than most of us do in our first. You said over lunch that this was a very exciting time to be an artist in Québec. What is it like?

CARRIER: It's quite simple. During lunch I compared the time we live in in Québec with the time a man becomes a man. Québec is growing and maturing, and we feel that we have a lot of things to do. It's fun to do them; everybody is really involved in a different experience. I speak about the writers: before 1960 writers did one book, or two, or three, and then they found a job and their literary work was finished because they had no good reason to continue; but here and now in Québec the young writers have the feeling that we are building the French-Canadian Québécois literature. It's an important time to do it. In doing it, we have the feeling of saving things from the past, and we have also the feeling of preparing what is coming. There are readers who wait for our books, who wait for our plays, with great interest. People read less and less French literature from France, and the main interest is in what is happening here in Québec. Even in France they know that their foreign literature is important; they become interested in it too. So writers feel that they are necessary, they are as useful as anybody, they are not outside of the society but they are in the society and they are an important part. In the schools the young students are very much interested in the past literature of Québec, that old literature that we don't know because of religious and political censorship; they discover those old authors with great pleasure, great interest, but they wait for the new authors. Often they buy books which are not yet published, they wait—and that's great! Writers here are people, we are workers, and we have a job to do which interests many people.

CAMERON: You're taking charge of the direction of Québec for yourselves intellectually and artistically as well.

CARRIER: No, I don't think we are taking charge, exactly. Other men have charge of Québec, stupid, incompetent men who love power. They have all the possibilities, the police and the army. I am trying to understand, to know what happened to our people. To know our people better, that is my job.

CAMERON: Do you get letters from your readers? Do people stop you in the street?

CARRIER: I have letters, but people don't stop a writer in the street: we have policemen to do that. I say that because of October 1970—but I have a kind of friendship with my readers. Very often I am invited to go to universities or go to schools and I have good discussions there, good conversations.

CAMERON: Do you think of yourself as an ambitious writer?

CARRIER: In life I have not very much ambition; I take things like they come. But literary ambition, yes.

CAMERON: You'd like to write the best damn novel of the century.

CARRIER: Yes. It's crazy, but that's the truth.

CAMERON: No, surely it's the only reason to write.

CARRIER: I am not that kind of guy who will meet important people to help him, that's not my kind of ambition. My kind of ambition is to do good books. The white page, that's where I want to be good. It's crazy.

CAMERON: It takes a long time. Do you brood about death? You often write of death.

CARRIER: I don't want to be anguished about that closing of the door. As long as the door is open, it's okay: let's go! If the door is smashed on my nose, what can I do? It's finished. In my novels, I speak many times about death, but that's not really myself; I speak about death because in our religious culture death was more important than life. Man was created, according to our religion, not to live but to die. The most important thing was death and the life after death, and that's why I speak so often of death, because for all the French Canadians death was the main thing, life after death. So they did not care about life during life. But my personal options are not concerned by that.

CAMERON: Is that why the comedy in your work is often macabre?

CARRIER: It's a way for me to mock at what we've learned. But it's comic yes and no. At the end of my third novel there is Philibert, who dies—maybe, maybe, I'm not sure, and the reader is not sure either. He dies in a car accident and dying— if he dies—he sees himself hurt. After that he sees himself in hell, and then a big snake comes and gets him in his mouth, and he goes down and gets out the back again. It's macabre, sure; it's maybe comic, because it's really too much; but at the same time it's quite anguishing, because I remember when I was a child and I know that that story's true. For every French Canadian the presence of the snake has menace, and is terrifying and horrible. We saw him in our dreams. It was the punishment against bad actions. It's macabre because our education showed us macabre things. We have to tell the truth about that, too.

September 13, 1971

Roch Carrier:
Biography and Bibliography

Roch Carrier was born in 1937 in St. Justin de Dorchester, a village in the Beauce region of Québec. After classical college and a master's degree from the Université de Montréal, he taught Greek culture for two years at Collège St. Louis in Edmundston, New Brunswick, before pursuing his studies at the Sorbonne. Returning to Canada in 1964, he taught for several years at the Université de Montréal. He is now resident dramatist with the Théâtre du Nouveau Monde in Montréal. With his wife and two daughters, he lives in Longueuil, Québec.

Fiction

Jolis Deuils (1967)
La Guerre, Yes Sir! (1968)
Floralie, Où Es Tu? (1969)
Contes Pour Mille Oreilles (1969)
Il Est Par Là, Le Soleil (1970)
La Guerre, Yes Sir! (dramatic version) (1971)

In English Translation:

La Guerre, Yes Sir! (1970)
Floralie, Where Are You? (1971)
Is It the Sun, Philibert? (1972)
Ellipse 4 (Summer, 1970) contains several stories from *Jolis Deuils* in translation.

Criticism

Georges-V. Fournier, "Roch Carrier: A Quest for the Authentic", Ellipse 4 (1970), 35-42. See also numerous reviews, especially of La Guerre, Yes Sir!

Robertson Davies :

The Bizarre and Passionate Life
of the Canadian People

Walking into the porter's lodge of Massey College in the University of Toronto, I was frightened. Robertson Davies, the Master of Massey College, is not only a sensitive and urbane novelist, but also an accomplished playwright, an exceptional journalist, a penetrating critic, a professional actor, a scholar, and an astringent wit. "Mr. Davies," A. J. M. Smith once wrote, "brings the virtues of urbanity, sophistication, good humour, and a certain consciousness of superiority to bear on books, food, wine and social behaviour." I greatly admired Davies' 1957 essay on Stephen Leacock, but I felt his Leacock anthology, Feast of Stephen, *was a waste of time; Davies in turn considered my* Faces of Leacock *altogether too earnestly academic; and both of us had published these opinions. I knew, too, that Davies was at the top of his powers: at fifty-eight, he had just published* Fifth Business, *by any standard the best novel he had ever written. I expected an ironic and uncomfortable afternoon.*

Inside Davies' study—a room so elegantly comfortable can hardly be called an office—I encountered someone considerably more rumpled, more round, and more quiet than the tall, suave, saturnine figure I had prepared for. I began asking questions suited to the man I thought he was, and got disconcerting answers. Was he a connoisseur of wine and cheese? No, he didn't know much about wine and didn't greatly enjoy cheese. Didn't the Salterton novels assume the reader and author agreed on the primary importance of social reality? No: consider the use of sermons, music, fantasy.

Confused, I resorted to the basic principle of good interviewing: when in doubt, shut your mouth and really listen. *I heard Davies saying that he was very different from his public image, and as I reshaped my view of him I found myself experiencing a deeply personal, almost confessional conversation.*

CAMERON: As I read them, the Salterton novels show a very strong feeling for the Western cultural tradition, and specifically the English tradition.

DAVIES: Well, I am interested in a lot of cultural traditions, as many as I can experience, really, but what is apparent in the Salterton novels is a Canadian cultural tradition which I don't think gets the kind of attention in Canadian fiction that it might expect: a sort of delayed cultural tradition. About the period that I was working on the Salterton novels, just after the 1945 war, there were still people living in places like Salterton whose tradition was directly Edwardian, and who saw nothing wrong with that. They weren't even conscious that their ideas were not contemporary. I remember driving with my wife from Peterborough to Cobourg to see a production of Chekhov's *The Cherry Orchard*, and in that very beautiful little theatre was an audience which contained a considerable number of people in evening dress, which I thought was very curious. They had come from that district, and they felt that that was the way that they ought to dress for a theatrical production. After the first act I wandered around in the corridors listening to the people talk, and they were talking about the play as if it were a brand-new play — because it *was* a brand-new play to most of them, and yet they were people of some education, of a very considerable amount of tradition; they had the kind of dress clothes that suggested that they were well accustomed to wearing them and had indeed been wearing them for a very long time. Suddenly it broke in upon me: these people don't know that the play is about *them* — and yet there it was. I knew who some of them were: they were descendants of people who'd come to this country in the middle of the nineteenth century or earlier; they had homes in which they used silver which their families had brought with them, they had pictures of Great-grandfather in his Bengal uniform, they had connections with England, cousins that they wrote to, and they still hadn't grasped the fact that an entirely new Canada had come into being, and that their sort of person was really almost dinosaur-like in its failure to fit into the modern scene. You could see what happened in *The Cherry Orchard* happening around there, because all kinds of places were having to be bought up, and people didn't quite know why, but somehow the money had run out. Canada is full of these people, and very rarely do they get written about, but I write about them, and they're *real*. I could lead you out on a walk within a mile of where we sit which would uncover a great many of them. This is something in Canada which people on the whole don't recognize: we've got a fantastic sort of fossilized past here. We always talk about ourselves as a country with a great future, but we never talk about ourselves as a country with a sort of living past.

CAMERON: Don't those novels show a fairly strong current of sympathy for some aspects of that tradition?

DAVIES: It is sympathy for the people — not, I think, the tradition — because they *are* people. They're not caricatures, they're not oddities, they're not cardboard. They bleed when you stick them and they weep when they are miserable, and their sorrows and their distresses are made sometimes more poignant by the fact that they don't know why things are happening to them.

CAMERON: The shape of the novels themselves is rather in the tradition of English domestic comedy, like Jane Austen or Henry James, in a way.

DAVIES: No. No, I've never read a novel by Henry James in my life, and I don't like Jane Austen. I agree with Max Beerbohm that the novels of Jane Austen are a marionette opera. I have no use for them whatever.

CAMERON: I'm becoming convinced I've misread you — but I thought there was an assumption in the Salterton novels of a kind of accepted social reality.

DAVIES: The people in the novels agree that there is a certain kind of reality; I don't think that should be taken as the *author's* opinion. In *A Mixture of Frailties* there are things which a lot of people who'd like the previous two novels disliked very much indeed, because it suggested that I and they had not agreed upon a kind of little provincial city which they could be cozy about it. *They* may have reached some such idea — but *I* never did.

CAMERON: You must have surprised them even more with *Fifth Business*.

DAVIES: Yes, and I hope to go on surprising them.

CAMERON: Are you working on a novel now?

DAVIES: Yes, and a great many people, I think, will find it uncongenial. Some people wrote to me and said that they liked *Fifth Business*, but it wasn't as funny as the other books. I'm grateful that they found the other books funny, but I am a little dismayed that they thought that funny was *all* they were. I think it is the writer's duty to be as amusing as he can manage, but not to sacrifice everything to that. That was what happened to Leacock: he eventually got so that he'd rather be funny than honest or sensible or intelligent, and that's bad.

CAMERON: Isn't it true that the comedy of the Salterton novels is a rather anguished comedy, too? That the reader is invited to feel for the character who is the butt of the comedy, as well as laughing at him?

DAVIES: Yes, he is the victim as well as the sort of originator. One of the things I was interested in doing when I wrote those novels was to try and find out whether such novels about Canada were possible, because I don't know of any others that deal with Canadian situations in quite that way — and yet they *are* Canadian. Many people said, Oh, I was trying to write as if Canada were England or as if I were an Englishman — but I'm *not* an Englishman, and Canada is *not* England, and English people found the books quite peculiar.

CAMERON: The play you mentioned in Cobourg was Russian. I've talked to novelists who've said that if some things that go on in Canada were written about accurately, the only parallel would be in Russian literature.

DAVIES: Exactly; I agree a hundred per cent. In fact sometimes I get irritated with people who complain that Canada has no drama. The two great Canadian dramatists are Chekhov and Ibsen. The Ibsen and Chekhov situations can be paralleled in Canada twenty times over — the same sort of rather uncomprehending clinging to the past on the part of a certain group of people, and the same sort of self-satisfied littleness of mind that you get savagely dealt with in so many of the Ibsen plays. What do the trolls tell Peer Gynt is their philosophy? Troll, to thyself be self-sufficient: now that's *Canadian*. We make modest faces sometimes to the rest of the world, but the hopeless self-satisfaction of a large number of Canadians is a marvel to behold.

CAMERON: I sense a good deal of Freudianism in your thinking. Is Freud someone you've read seriously and thought about a lot?

DAVIES: Yes, I have, as a matter of fact. I am, I guess, one of the very few people I know who has read Freud's collected works from end to end. Freud was an enormous enthusiasm of mine before I was forty; after forty I came to examine the works of his great colleague Carl Gustav Jung, and I have been, over many years, reading and re-reading and reading again the collected works of C. G. Jung.

CAMERON: What gave you that serious an interest in psychoanalytic thought in the first place?

DAVIES: Well, I had been interested in the notion that this line of thought existed even when I was a schoolboy; when I went to Queen's University there was a remarkable professor of psychology there, Dr. George Humphrey, a notable man who later on became Professor of Psychology at Oxford and wrote a great book on the theory of learning. Humphrey talked a great deal about Freud, about whom he knew a lot, and so I was led to read some Freud. One of the things that enchanted me was that Freud was saying explicitly things which I had vaguely apprehended as possibilities. This whetted my appetite enormously, so on I went. Later on I discovered the same thing in Jung: he had had the intellect and the ability to go into very deeply, and to talk about superbly, things which I had dimly apprehended, and so I was eager to follow.

CAMERON: Was there something that you became unsatisfied with in Freud?

DAVIES: Yes, there was. It was Freud's reductive train of thought, which is very welcome to the young mind but becomes, I find, less welcome to the older mind. Freud didn't indulge in this kind of thing, but a great many of his disciples do: you're afraid of thunder because when you were little you heard your father fart and then he spanked you, or something of that sort. Well, this seems to me unworthy of the human race. It's not the kind of cheap wares in which Freud dealt, but it's a thing that people have rather developed from his line of thinking, and much of his thought *is* violently reductive—the tendency to feel that the sexual etiology of neurosis explains everything, and that sort of thing. As Jung pointed out, a surprising number of people seemed to turn up in Jung's consulting room with manifest neuroses which were not primarily related to any sort of sexual hangup. As Jung also pointed out, Freud was an extraordinarily brilliant and very, very successful young man—the darling of his doting mother—who had always lived a city life. Jung had led much more the kind of childhood I myself had had—going to country schools, living with country children, knowing country things, being quite accustomed to animals and the sort of rough and rather sexually oriented—but in an ordinary, daily way—life of the country person.

CAMERON: Robert Kroetsch, who lives in the States, feels that Freudianism had great success there because it really appeals to something in American experience, in American ideology: the stress between the good guy and the bad guy, the id and the ego, a kind of Manichean view of the psyche.

DAVIES: That's extremely interesting.

CAMERON: And he felt that Canada was a much more Jungian society.

DAVIES: Ooooh, this is music to my soul! I think we're a much softer-focussed country. In the intellectual life of the United States, there seems to be such a very, very strong Jewish strain —I would not for an instant suggest that that was a bad thing, but it is an intensely *conditioning* thing. This intellectual ferocity and sort of black/white quality is very strong there. We're fuzzier, but I think we're more humane, and that's what I think about Jung, too.

CAMERON: Kroetsch thinks that instead of seeing polar oppositions all the time, we tend to see two sides of a conflict as aspects
of the same thing.

DAVIES: Yes, and tending to run into one another. You know, we
had a very extraordinary evidence of that, in something which
I think of as enormously important and significant about
Canada: in the character of Mackenzie King, who was our
Prime Minister for longer than any other man in any British
country in the world. Mackenzie King seemed to be the
quintessence of dullness. When you read in his diary that when
he met Barbara Ann Scott, the skater, it seemd that he was
expected to kiss her, and he "acquiesced"—a duller, more
pedantic, dreary man you could scarcely think to find. But
what was he in reality? A man who communed with the portrait of his dead mother to get political advice; a man who
never set the date of a general election without consulting
Nan Skinner, the Kingston fortune-teller; a man who could
—and I know this from my father, who knew Mr. King quite
well—burst into the most highly coloured and inflammatory
kind of blasphemous, evil language when he was discussing
certain topics; a man who wooed and sort of managed to keep
peace with Québec, but who could talk about French Canadians in a way that would take the paint off a barn door—this
was Mackenzie King, this was the opposites running into
one another, and this is very Canadian. We now blackmouth
him and pretend that we knew about him all the time, but he
got elected over and over again; he knew this country marvellously, because he was essentially one of us. We're great
withholders, Canadians. This is the sort of thing that my
Australian-born wife has pointed out to me. Accept the bland,
quiet, rather dull Canadian for what he seems to be: it's just
like putting your hand into a circular saw, he'll have the hand
before you know what's happened. I think this is very characteristic of our country, and when we really come to ourselves,
we're going to be a very formidable people. We're going to be

as formidable, I would say, as the Norwegians, or the Swedes, who are very formidable nations indeed; perhaps as formidable as the Russians. I was asked in connection with *Fifth Business* to say what I was trying to do, and I said that I was trying to record the bizarre and passionate life of the Canadian people. Well, I was dropped on by some Canadian critics who said, There I was again, trying to make an effect and talking silly so that people would look at me and think what a fancy fellow I was. *They* were the ones who didn't see what it was. I was speaking the exact truth, but they didn't see it. They *will not* see it.

CAMERON: As you spoke, I thought, This is the theme of *Fifth Business*, the contrast between —

DAVIES: — the appearance and the reality, the grey schoolmaster and the man who was burning like an oil gusher inside.

CAMERON: Yes, and at a place much like Upper Canada College, which many people consider the epitome of all that is dull and Edwardian.

DAVIES: You see, they don't know anything about it. I went to Upper Canada College, and I know what a tempest of passion can go on in there. I'm not saying it's individual to that college; it would be so in any school in Canada, I would think, if you just look. Some very rum things indeed go on in them. Every once in a while a teacher commits suicide, and everyone says, "Poor old Joe, you wouldn't have thought it of him, would you? He seemed to be the most level-headed fellow there ever was." But if you knew old Joe, you knew old Joe had been nutty as a fruit cake for years. I went to a collegiate institute for a while where there was a mathematics teacher who used to break down in the class sometimes; he would burst into tears and say, "Children, I don't want to die of cancer, I don't want to die of cancer." He eventually did — he wasn't doing it at that moment — but we just thought, well, that's the way old Scotty is. The goddamndest things go on in schools.

CAMERON: How on earth did you get that astonishing report of the experience of a foot soldier in the First World War? You were all of one year old when the war broke out.

DAVIES: I wish I could give you some helpful and illuminating answer, but I can't. I just remember when I was a very little boy what some men who were in the war had said. They weren't very eloquent, but it was like that. But I will tell you something which is not dissimilar. In *Fifth Business* I mentioned that the Bollandists, and particularly Padre Blazon, wrote in purple ink. Well, I've never seen a Bollandist, and I think I've only met one Jesuit, and I've never visited the Bollandist Institute in Brussels, or anything of that sort, but I did meet a man in New York called Israel Shenker, who knows the Bollandists very well and is, as far as a layman and a visitor can be, a familiar there. And he said, How on earth did you know that they wrote in purple ink? I said, Well, I divined it—and he nearly fell out of his chair with indignation, because this was a bad answer. But it seemed to me very probable that they would write in purple ink, and apparently they do.

CAMERON: But you didn't check.

DAVIES: How would you check? Would you write to them and say, Please, do you write in purple ink? It isn't a matter of importance, really. I could have just said that they wrote in ink. But it seemed to me—welllllll, *purple* ink. And they do.

CAMERON: That's quite a chance to take. Certain kinds of reviewers would be very indignant if they were to find out that in fact it was green ink.

DAVIES: Yes, they would. They'd be very cross.

CAMERON: The religious theme that emerged so strongly in *Fifth Business* had been seen primarily in social terms, I would have thought, in the Salterton novels.

DAVIES: Yes, but not entirely in social terms. In *Leaven of Malice*, the Dean makes it pretty clear what his view is about what has been going on, and puts in his ten cents' worth in a way I hoped was of some significance. Only a very few people have ever commented on the Dean's sermon at the very end of *A Mixture of Frailties*, which is going on contrapuntally to what the girl Monica is thinking when she's trying to make up her mind whether she'll marry Domdaniel or not. The Dean is preaching a sermon on the revelation of God to man in three forms: a revolution of nature for the shepherd, a penetration by wisdom for the wise man, and a sort of natural grace to Simeon. I think most people look at the italics and say, Oh yes, this is the sermon, and hop to where it gets to be roman type next, to see whether the girl's going to marry the old man or not. But it's there, and it's vital to the book.

CAMERON: Has religion something to do with your interest in Freud and Jung?

DAVIES: Yes. One reason I was drawn to the study of Freud and of Jung was my religious interest, because I very quickly found that for my taste, investigation of religion by orthodox theological means was unrewarding. You never got down to brass tacks, or at least nothing that I ever read did so. You started off by assuming that certain things were true, and then you developed all kinds of splendid things on top of that. I wanted to see about the basic things, so I thought that I would have a look at people who had had a wrestle with these very, very basic things, and Freud was one of them. Freud decided that religion is essentially an illusion: well, I read that, I studied it and chewed on it and mulled it over for quite a long time, but it never fully satisfied me, because it seemed to me that brilliant as Sigmund Freud was, there have been men of comparable brilliance or even greater brilliance who had been enormously attached to this concept which seemed to him to be nothing better than an illusion. One of the figures which bulked very large in my ideas was St. Augustine. I was very interested as a very young boy to discover that I was born on the day of St. Augustine, the 28th of August, and also on the birthday of Tolstoy and Goethe; and I thought, Oh, that's great stuff, splendid! This is an omen. But St. Augustine was a man of the most towering intellectual powers, and if he was willing to devote his life to the exposition of this thing which Freud called an illusion, I felt that the betting couldn't all be on Saint Sigmund; some of it conceivably ought to be on St. Augustine. And there were other figures whom I thought intensely significant. I thought a great deal

about it, and then I gradually began to look into the works of
Jung and found a much more—to me—satisfying attitude towards religion, but it was not an orthodox Christian one. Orthodox Christianity has always had for me the difficulty that
it really won't come, in what is for me a satisfactory way, to
grips with the problem of evil. It knows an enormous
amount about evil, it discusses evil in fascinating terms, but
evil is always the other thing: it is something which is apart
from perfection, and man's duty is to strive for perfection. I
could not reconcile that with such experience of life as I had,
and the Jungian feeling that things tend to run into one another,
that what looks good can be pushed to the point where it becomes evil, and that evil very frequently bears what can only
be regarded as good fruit—this was the first time I'd ever seen
that sort of thing given reasonable consideration, and it made
enormous sense to me. I feel now that I am a person of strongly
religious temperament, but when I say "religious" I mean im-
mensely conscious of powers of which I can have only the
dimmest apprehension, which operate by means that I cannot
fathom, in directions which I would be a fool to call either
good or bad. Now that seems hideously funny, but it isn't
really; it is, I think, a recognition of one's position in an in-
explicable universe, in which it is not wholly impossible for
you to ally yourself with, let us say, positive rather than neg-
ative forces, but in which anything that you do in that direction must be done with a strong recognition that you may be
very, very gravely mistaken. This is something which would
never satisfy the humblest parish priest, but I live in a world in
which forces are going on which I am unable to tab and
identify so that the tickets will stick. I just have to get on as
well as I can. Various kind people in writing about my books
have called me an existentialist, and they won't believe me
when I tell them I don't know what an existentialist is. I've had
it explained to me many times, but the explanation never really
makes enough sense to me to cling. But I have tried to state for
you what my position is, and I fear that I've done so clumsily

and muddily—but if it comes in clumsy and muddy, it's just got to be that way. Better that than slick and crooked.

CAMERON: Perhaps people find it difficult to believe that you don't know what an existentialist is because of your public *persona*, your image, to use the ad-man's word, which—

DAVIES: —my image, if I've got an image—I suppose I have —has been made for me by other people. Nobody wants to listen to what I want to say. They want to tell me what I think.

CAMERON: Well, the image presents you as a man of formidable learning, formidable intellect, and fearsome wit, a man who *would* know about things like existentialism.

DAVIES: I am not of formidable learning; I am a very scrappily educated person, and I am not of formidable intellect; I really am not a very good thinker. In Jungian terms I am a feeling person with strong intuition. I *can* think, I've *had* to think, and I *do* think, but thinking isn't the first way I approach any problem. It's always, What does this say to me? And I get it through my fingertips, not through my brain. *Then* I have to think about it, but the thinking is a kind of consciously undertaken thing rather than a primary means of apprehension. Also intuition is very strong in me; I sort of smell things. As for this wit business, it's primarily defence, you know. Witty people are concealing something.

CAMERON: What are you concealing?

DAVIES: I suppose I'm concealing—hmmm. Well, you see, if it were easy for me to tell you, I wouldn't be concealing. I think I am concealing a painful sensitivity, because I am very easily hurt and very easily rebuffed and very easily set down; and very early in life I found out that to be pretty ready with your tongue was a way of coping with that. You know that is a thing which is attributed to Dunstan Ramsay in *Fifth Business*. He was always "getting off a good one". If you can get off a good one once or twice a day, people don't rasp you as much as they otherwise might. They'll do it enough, however defensive you are.

CAMERON: Humour does fend people off.

DAVIES: It's defensive and it's diverting. You know, you suddenly send the dogs off in that direction, instead of straight ahead.

CAMERON: One can't talk about these things as a dispassionate interviewer, you know. I've been known in some circles as a person of fairly savage humour myself, and I've always felt that in my case it had to do with profound feelings of insecurity and inadequacy, the sense that I was surrounded by people who knew their way around the world and were at home in it in a way that I wasn't.

DAVIES: Yes, there's that, and there's also a thing which I expect you have experienced, and which certainly I've experienced: the narrow outlook, and limited sympathies, and want of charity, and general two-bit character of what is going on under your very eyes, which drives you to the point of great extravagance. It comes out in terms of savage, bitter humour, just because you don't quite want to go to savage denunciation, but you want to blast them like an Old Testament prophet. Instead you just swat them around with the jester's bladder. But the impulse is the same.

CAMERON: Isn't the effect actually more powerful through humour, and isn't that something else one easily learns?

DAVIES: Yes, but you haven't learned enough. If you blasted them like a prophet, they might forgive you; if you mock them like a jester, they'll *never* forgive you.

CAMERON: That's true, but it's because making a joke of them is a more powerful thing to do.

DAVIES: Yes, I guess it is, in a way. Oh, it hurts, it stings, and they never forgive it. Now this is interesting: you have made a confession and I've made one. That's why one makes jokes, very often.

CAMERON: To make confessions—?

DAVIES: No, to keep things at bay. It's a sort of distancing thing very often. Not always: I mean, sometimes you do it out of sheer lark.

CAMERON: There's a very interesting interplay in your work

between theatre and fiction. I suspect that for you theatre is a metaphor of some dimensions.

DAVIES: It's the element of illusion in life, the difference between appearance and reality. In the theatre you can be in the know about what makes the difference, and it is fascinating that you can know what creates the illusion, know everything about it, be part of it, and yet not despise the people who want the illusion, who cannot live without it. That's important, you know. So frequently it is assumed that if you know how something's done you despise the people who don't. You don't do that in the theatre. You respect them; you know that they know a good thing when they see it.

CAMERON: You were with the Old Vic at one point, weren't you?

DAVIES: Yes, not for very long. For three years, until the war broke out and there was nothing further to be done there or anywhere else in England, so I came back to Canada.

CAMERON: You are very strongly Canadian, aren't you, in that you have a very clear sense of who you are and which national community is yours.

DAVIES: Yes, indeed, and this became very very clear to me within the last two or three years. I've always felt strongly Canadian, which doesn't mean complacently or gleefully Canadian, but Canadian; and my father, who was a Welshman, had always, during the latter part of his life, spent all his summers in his native country, in Wales. My mother was Canadian and her family had been here for a very long time — since 1785 as a matter of fact — but my father always had this extraordinary pull back to his home country. Living in this college, I live in a house which is attached to the college, which is not mine, and when I retire I will not, of course, continue to live there. So my wife and I thought the time had come when we ought to have some place where we'll be able to go when we retire. Distant though that time may be, now is the time to get on with doing it, because when you're retired you don't want to plunge right into the business of finding a dwelling or building one. So we thought, what'll we do? Will we acquire some place in England and retire there? Now this would have been comprehensible because there was this very strong pull of my father's towards the old land, and my wife's family, who were Australians, were always drawn back to England as the great, good place in which all important things happened. We talked it over and decided that my wife had been a Canadian far longer than she'd been an Australian, and that I was really a Canadian, and that to leave this country would be like cutting off my feet. So we built a house in the country in Canada. That was a decision which went far beyond a matter of bricks and mortar. It would be impossible now to leave with the feeling that you'd left for good. We like to travel, we like to get around to see what's doing, we're both terribly interested in the theatre, which means we like to get over to England where the theatre is most lively, and to the continent. But to live, to have your being, to feel that this is where you're going to get old and die, that's another thing—and that's *here*.

CAMERON: That doesn't surprise me now, but it might have before I met you.

DAVIES: Well, as we've said, the popular notion of what I am and why I do things is very wide of the mark. The mainstream of what I do is this sense which I can only call a religious sense, but which is not religious in a sectarian, or aggressive, or evangelistic sense. And also, you know, I really think I've now got to the age where I have to consider what I am and how I function, and I can only call myself an artist. Now people hesitate very much in Canada to call themselves artists. An extraordinary number of authors shrink from that word, because it suggests to them a kind of fancy attitude, which might bring laughter or might seem overstrained—but if you really put your best energies into acts of creation, I don't know what else you can call yourself. You'd better face it and get used to it, and take on the things that are implied by it.

CAMERON: What sorts of things are implied?

DAVIES: A duty to be true to your abilities in so far as

you can and as deeply as you can. I think this is where Leacock didn't trust himself, didn't trust his talent. He never thought of himself as an artist, which he started out, I'm sure, to be; his early work has a lot of that quality about it. He decided he was going to be a moneymaker instead, so he didn't become the writer he might have been, and I think that's what you've got to do if you have a chance. I couldn't have said this until fairly recently — you know, you step out in front of the public and say, I am an artist, and they shout, Yeah? Look who's talking, and throw eggs. If you step out in front of them and say, I am a humorist, they say, All right, make us laugh. You can do that fairly easily, but if you say, I can make you feel; I can maybe even make you cry, that's claiming a lot.

CAMERON: And do they want you to do it?

DAVIES: They really do, but they want to be sure that they're in safe hands before they let you do it, because you might be kidding them: you might make them cry and then say, Yah, yah, look who's crying; I did that as a trick — and that's what would hurt them. They're sensitive too. It's an awareness of approaching and retreating sensibilities that is not very easy to acquire.

CAMERON: W. O. Mitchell refers to the reader as a "creative partner".

DAVIES: *Yes!* Exactly! And you've got to find the way to make it possible for him to create without being ashamed of himself afterwards. Only an artist can do that.

November 9, 1971

Robertson Davies:
Biography and Bibliography

Robertson Davies was born in Thamesville, Ontario, in 1913, and educated at Upper Canada College, Queen's University, and Balliol College, Oxford. He was associated with the Old Vic theatre company in London as actor and literary assistant for three years before returning to Canada as literary editor of Saturday Night. *He then became, for twenty years, editor of the Peterborough* Examiner, *where he first published many of the Samuel Marchbanks sketches. In 1963 he was appointed Professor of English and Master of Massey College in the University of Toronto, the position he now holds. He holds honorary degrees from six universities, and has been awarded the Lorne Pierce Medal of the Royal Society of Canada for distinguished contributions to Canadian literature. Married, with three daughters, Professor Davies makes his home in Toronto.*

Fiction

The Diary of Samuel Marchbanks (1947)
The Table Talk of Samuel Marchbanks (1949)
Samuel Marchbanks' Almanack (1967)
Tempest-Tost (1951)
Leaven of Malice (1954)
A Mixture of Frailties (1958)
Fifth Business (1970)
The Manticore (1972)

Plays

Eros at Breakfast, and Other Plays (1949)

Fortune My Foe (1949)
At My Heart's Core (1950)
A Masque of Aesop (1952)
A Jig for the Gypsy (1954)
A Masque of Mr. Punch (1963)
Four Favourite Plays (collection) (1968)
Hunting Stuart and Other Plays (1972)

Non-Fiction

Shakespeare's Boy Actors (1939)
A Voice from the Attic (1960)
Feast of Stephen (1970; long introduction separately published as *Stephen Leacock*, 1970)

In Collaboration with Sir Tyrone Guthrie:

Renown at Stratford (1953)
Twice Have The Trumpets Sounded (1954)
Thrice The Brinded Cat Hath Mew'd (1955)

Criticism

Elspeth Fisher Buitenhuis, Robertson Davies (1972)
Gordon Roper, Robertson Davies *(forthcoming)*

Timothy Findley:

Make Peace With Nature, Now

Late June, and the wide rolling hills northeast of Toronto begin to yellow. Flies buzz, a blind old cat walks across a picnic table. Timothy Findley lifts her gently to the ground, and she meanders off past the ornamental pond and along the stone wall.

The garden is large, informal, but lovingly tended. The brick farmhouse melts into the landscape; fifty acres of fields rise softly behind it, with a new barn growing in the foreground, a bricklayer slopping mortar near its base. Several teen-aged boys skitter about on top of the house, repairing the roof. Their sounds are muted in the warm, still air.

Across the table, Timothy Findley is talking, a boyishly good-looking man of forty. Extraordinarily soft-spoken and considerate, Findley's manner contrasts eerily with the apocalyptic passion of what he is saying. We have destroyed nature, he declares, we are destroying ourselves, the human experiment is ending. Bill Whitehead, the CBC science reporter, crosses the lawn with a tray of tea and cakes.

If he had a samovar, the scene would be complete, for the ghost in the gooseberry bushes is that of Chekhov. Findley began as an actor, working in New York and London (and Stratford) with Alec Guinness, Tyrone Guthrie, and Peter Brook, among others. Thornton Wilder and Ruth Gordon encouraged him to write, and he has done films, radio, and television — including the Jalna scripts — as well as fiction. The controlled melody of his voice is an actor's resource which he still uses in his regular talks on CBC radio. Fiction and theatre, and this atmosphere: yes, it must be Chekhov. And then there is the name he and Bill have given to their house.

They call it The Stone Orchard.

CAMERON: You're very concerned about man's relation to nature.

FINDLEY: Yes, I have a motto, which is "Make peace with nature, now." I really believe that we're at war with nature, and we have declared war on a defenceless enemy. I hope I'm not misanthropic, because I love many human beings, but I'm afraid I'm not particularly fond of the human race.

CAMERON: Jonathan Swift said almost exactly that, once.

FINDLEY: Did he? Maybe I had read it and subconsciously remembered—but the thing is, it's the arrogance, Don. Who are we to say that we're the end product of all this? How do we know that the frogs aren't the things that are going to end up being the sum total of evolution? We have no way of knowing; we think we have ways of knowing, but how do we know that as things evolve the planet isn't headed for some kind of atmosphere where bees are the thing that are really evolving? Perhaps man is almost done evolving. And in fact this is the subject of my next novel. Not scientifically, because I'm dreary on science—Bill Whitehead, with whom I live, is a brilliant scientist, but not an academic scientist, so I listen to him. I can't write it, I can't talk it, but I understand it in my bones, what is happening to us. I really think that we have gone beyond the meaning of civilization. We have accomplished all that civilization can accomplish, and all that is left is waste and meaningless.

CAMERON: There's something of your pro-nature quality in Hooker Winslow in *The Last of the Crazy People*.

FINDLEY: I think Hooker is a saviour figure, by which I don't mean at all anything Christ-like. There are people who come to save and people who come to destroy, and it's funny how Hooker winds up killing the family. It evolved absolutely against my will: one night I was upstairs writing and came down in floods of tears because I had discovered that this was the only thing that he could do. You would imagine, I'm sure, that the book had been written from the very first word in the knowledge that that was what was going to happen—it wasn't. At first I thought that perhaps he went downstairs into the cellar and killed his cats, and then about two days after that I realized that that isn't what he did, that he had to save the family by ending their lives, ending their misery. It was the only thing that he could do—and all the other things in the book had pointed to it. Then, of course, there was some reorganizing to do, in terms of having come upon this thing. The very beginning did get rewritten, and all that kind of thing.

CAMERON: The little prologue *had* to be written after that.

FINDLEY: Right, it was written at the end. But when I was young, I had a friend, and this is what he did. He didn't, thank God, get all the way to killing all his family, but he did kill his mother and his sister and then — but boy! I'll never forget sitting in that room and having that thing just overwhelm me, the knowledge that that was what he had to do.

CAMERON: What Hooker had to do.

FINDLEY: Yeah. They become very, very real to you, Don. I don't know whether you've found in your talks with other writers how real their people are to them. But in *The Butterfly Plague*, after Naomi died, I couldn't work for two weeks; although I knew she was going to, it was like a personal loss, it's that kind of thing. It's vicious being a writer. Along with all the other impossible things, such as the loneliness and the lack of security — not just financial security, either — one of the worst things is the inner demand that you be a professional. You have to be a professional. You have to be utterly disciplined about whatever you're doing, which is to say you have to make yourself do the thing your integrity has told you is the right thing to do, despite all the fearful and cautionary advice you get from your mind. All authors are whispered to by their characters. The characters want life, and you have to give it to them. It's a little like rape, with no recourse to abortion. They take your body, and you have to give birth. So "professionalism" is obedience, to be obedient to the whispering inside of you, among other things. That's one of the great disciplines, and the others, naturally, have to do with making yourself work and so on.

CAMERON: What were you tempted to say about the lack of security?

FINDLEY: The lack of security is that you're sitting alone and you can't verify anything that you feel with anyone. You can't go to anyone and say, Is this right? You can only consult yourself on these matters. No one in the whole world understands you as you are in the process of creation. There's no way anyone *can* understand you, because you can barely understand yourself. My analogy is always this: that I'm lying somewhere, and in my mind someone will walk up in blue, carrying a suitcase, and their mouth is set in a certain way, and their fingers are doing something. They stand there in a particular way and they will not go away. And you turn your eyes this way and you turn your eyes that way, and they're there. They're *there*. And this is how what writing is begins. They arrive on your doorstep, and they say, I am coming into your life and I am not going to leave until I am down on the paper and that's the end of it.

CAMERON: Some writers have confidence in somebody other than themselves, usually a wife. I don't know if they would defer in the last analysis, if there were really serious disagreement.

FINDLEY: Oh, I think you don't ever defer in the last analysis, if the battle has been long and hard. This is what Bill Whitehead is to me, no question. But you're talking about a later stage of affairs. I'm talking about the agonies—they can only be described as that. You're being torn asunder! I'm sorry to be so melodramatic about it, but this is really what it's like—and I want to get that thing across. People say, Well, why are all these writers drunk all the time? and why are they always so sad and why are they so angry? and why do they always want to be by themselves? and why are they always so nasty when you come to the door, and blah blah blah blah. They really do wonder why we're like that. Why did Faulkner hide in that house, why did he do that? Why, *why* do we have to jump and talk when he wants to talk? You wonder how many times people allowed themselves to sit down and listen to the man when he finally decided he had something to say. It must have saved him millions of times from suicide. It's that ghastly. You're always on the point of suicide. It's a very melodramatic thing to say, but if it's true, if it is what you *are*, if it's not an act and if it's not sophisticated and if it's not—forgive me for saying this to an academic but I know you'll understand what

I mean when I say this — as long as it doesn't become academic and therefore a learned thing, instead of a natural thing. There is much to learn, but it isn't by an education, you see. There is the discipline, there are all the ordered things about work and writing and structure and pace. At the same time I think most of those things have to come to you naturally and what you're really learning is how to select. My biggest problem as a writer is the fear of not having made a thing clear, and I'll write the same thing into a novel several times so that by the time I've got it said, I've said it eight different ways, through eight different characters. I must learn that I don't need to do that. I'm still not trusting. I don't trust enough — either myself or the reader.

CAMERON: I noticed that repetition in particular in *The Butterfly Plague*.

FINDLEY: At some point when you're writing anything, you get mixed up with your editors or you get mixed up with your producer if it's television or radio. They'll ask for clarification of various things. In some cases they're right to ask for clarification of something that is so personal that you feel it hasn't needed to be explained — you know, why somebody has black dots at the end of their fingers — but in *The Butterfly Plague* I got into the greatest hassle when the editor kept saying, But you must explain what the butterflies mean. And I got in the most terrible panic about that, because of course they meant everything. They were the people who had flocked to California, they were fascists, they were the people who were being destroyed by the fascists, both the Jews and the Germans, they were *everything*. They were anything you wanted them to be. Please don't make me put that on paper, I said, don't pin it down for God's sake, but I wrote two sentences, at their demand, and it ruined the whole book for me.

CAMERON: Earlier today you described a certain kind of sea as being beautiful and sinister, and the butterflies are certainly like that. That's a combination of qualities your work often presents.

FINDLEY: I don't work for it, but I recognize that it's there. What I don't know,.and what's probably interesting to speculate about is, Is what is sinister beautiful? Or is what is beautiful sinister? And that is where the balance is interesting.

CAMERON: What would your own speculations be?

FINDLEY: I know that my speculations would be that what is beautiful is sinister, rather than what is sinister is beautiful, because I have no overt sadism in me and I have no overt masochism. The balance in me I think is fairly even. I am not a masochist and I am not a sadist in the given sense of either of those words. I have a little of both in me, but I'm sure as hell not sadistic enough to really think that anything sinister is beautiful. But at the same time, this funny thing always rises up in me, which is the thing about insanity. There's always someone who must do insane things in order to clarify what, for want of better words, is bright and good. Hooker had to murder in order to achieve peace for those people, in order to demonstrate his love for them. Ruth had to be maddened and thought insane — I mean it's so awful, that's what was so awful about that book to me. I'm closest to her, therefore I probably haven't got her down as well as I would like to have got her down. But it's that sense in her that she has seen the most terrible things that can be seen, and heard the most horrible things that can be heard, and been made to do the most horrible things that can be done, and everyone thinks *she's* crazy. But they accept all these people actually being shunted off to death camps — what's wrong with that?

CAMERON: You told me earlier that you had a very interesting childhood in a lot of ways, but that you didn't think I wanted to hear about it. Well, I do.

FINDLEY: I know what you want me to throw light on, and I don't know how to throw light on it. Where did Hooker come from, and is it me? I did have strange relationships with all the people in my childhood. I had no interest in other children, maybe because I was often sick and had no tie to what other kids were doing. Whenever I went out to play, I'd tag along after my older brother and, quite naturally, he didn't want me hanging around his neck everywhere he went. Consequently I often ended up back with the adults. I spent a lot of time with the maid, or just plain by myself, so it got that I sort of feared other kids. I was like Hooker Winslow in that I was fairly often alone, maybe aloof. And if I had a friend, we got on strangely. I was never pals with anybody. I had a couple of good friends, but there was a strangeness about it. Nothing but surface communication. I was sent to a boarding school during the worst part of the war, and I remember all of that as being coloured brown, all that part of my life. I hated the other kids in that school—Jesus, talk about male chauvinist pigs! And my brother got sick; he had rheumatic fever and he nearly died and I was left there all by myself and my mother could hardly ever come to see me. Dad was at war and I just felt— abandoned. Oh God, it was just ghastly. Awful experiences like that.

CAMERON: What caught my attention in *The Last of the Crazy People* wasn't just Hooker, but also that sense of the whole family working within a very exacting and very obscure set of rules and procedures peculiar to themselves.

FINDLEY: I think all of those people in essence exist. Of course, with all writing, you take the things that exist, you add a few more things from other people, and then you take it to its creative conclusion. But my father was enormously preoccupied with my older brother, just as Nick is in the book with Gilbert. There's a lot of my older brother in Gilbert, but there's a hell of a lot of me in Gilbert too. I remember being terribly upset by my brother's reaction to the book—he hated me having put anything on paper that even approximated what he was like, and that just broke my heart because you see all of those portraits in that book to me really are drawn with a loving hand, which surely anybody would recognize. They're not vindictive or vitriolic portraits. On the other hand I don't want to vindicate myself by making statements like that; the book is what it is. And the truths in that book are there because they exist, out of my experience; there's no point in denying that at all.

CAMERON: Why are we getting so many novels recently which are very concerned with Nazism?

FINDLEY: Well, you got a lot of big books about the war, and about the concentration camps, which hadn't to do with politics. It's just now that we're geting back to the place where we recognize, through repetition, how that *other* thing happened. There's no question that what is happening in Washington right now is the result of having walked for about ten years in the direction of fascism. If you think about the people who are now in jail in the States you can't help but draw the analogy. All the same words are being used: honour, place, stature, honesty, right, and so forth, and the same horrifying things are being done in the name of all these beautiful words. We've been very arrogant about our attitude towards the German people, and we've said things like, How could you possibly live in that country and not know what was going on? But all through the 1940s the Americans were building up towards the creation of the atomic bomb. They created it, they developed it, they exploded it, and they dropped it—*and the people did not know*.

CAMERON: Several of the novelists I've talked to are talking about The Revolution. They mean all kinds of different things by The Revolution, but there's just no doubt in any of their minds—

FINDLEY: —we're in it now. My part of the revolution has got to do with nature. I can remember being laughed at for saying this as short a while ago as four years—I don't think I'd be laughed at now—that you can't bring up children with the attitude that they may pick up a gun and wander into the field and kill anything at random, and not expect to have the end product of that be the massacre at My Lai. I didn't have the example of My Lai four years ago; I used Viet Nam in general. But there are people who can't wait to get to Viet Nam and "kill the gooks". The famous American story about this is that the gun is the great equalizer; you have a right to this. We have a right to go armed against nature. That's how it begins, and the next thing you know, you're armed against your fellow man. Compassion is one of the first things that people try to eradicate in children. I know this about my own childhood— they tried to get it out of me and I consciously refused. I was told not to speak kindly to the maid, and if a little old man came to the door and wanted twenty-five cents I was told that he was a dirty little old man and that I mustn't stand there at the door talking to him. But I was told that in all innocence; my mother and father weren't evil. It was inculcated into their very fibre that you did not do that, just as you *did* take your son out hunting. There's one kid who goes down the road here very unhappily every spring and fall with his father in the car. Every time anything moves in the field over there, the kid is told to get out of the car and go and kill it, or try. And the kid doesn't want to do it.

CAMERON: Does that have to do with things like the urge for mastery that goes into industrialization? Fishing is just a little different, but hunting, I think, seems particularly to attract certain kinds of aggressive businessmen.

FINDLEY: They've mastered something—they haven't, of course. I do acknowledge that among fishermen, of all those who hunt, you find the only gentlemen. Gentle men. Because they're the only ones who do put the prey back into its element on occasion. And a great many fishermen do catch it and put it back. But you can't put an animal back, you can't put a tree back if you've cut it down, you can't put a bird back if you've shot it out of the goddamn sky. What we have done to the human race is to brutalize it beyond all recognition of what the human race—I won't say, is meant to be, because that predicates some kind of belief in God which I don't think I have. I have a belief in a being that is all of nature, though. But we found the greatest possibilities, they exist in the Michelangelos and the Beethovens and so on, and we've turned away from them, having exhausted that. Now all we have left is to brutalize the human spirit.

CAMERON: Do you foresee any turn away from that brutalization?

FINDLEY: No, I don't. I'm afraid I really see nothing but that—I think it's my responsibility to say what I really believe is going to happen: that we have come to the parting of the ways, and from here on in we're something else—which is not going to be a pleasant being at all.

CAMERON: Some rough beast, its hour come round at last.

FINDLEY: Right.

CAMERON: I'm so depressed I'll change the subject. You've been a professional actor: have you tried to write plays?

FINDLEY: Yes, I'm moving towards that very gradually and with a great deal of fear—because I have this fear, which is the fear of the market place, and I had it as an actor, which I'm sure is why I ended up with ulcers instead of joy. I should have written about eighty-five plays by now and had maybe one produced, but I'm just approaching the place where the first play that I've really cared about is about to be produced on radio. I'm treating that in my mind as, We are now in Boston approaching the first rewrites but we're not going to know what the rewrites are until we've given this one performance on radio. It's a play I believe in very strongly and very much want something to happen to. It'll be done, as it is in Boston, in public, and all the mistakes are going to be screaming out at everybody out loud, but it's the only way to learn. Then I'll rewrite it according to what went wrong, and I know a great deal will go wrong—because you don't know until you get actors doing it and things happening, and then you know you've said too much here and too little there and so on, and then I want to rewrite it from that point of view. Then I hope to get it on a stage and find out again what's wrong, and so forth. I love the theatre and I have another play in my mind, so I always think of myself as being a play-writer and a novelist, whether the facts are such or not. I've written a lot of screenplays and I think like that, in a natural way.

CAMERON: What do cats mean to you? Hooker has all those cats in *The Last of the Crazy People*, and then I come here and find you have eighteen cats.

FINDLEY: They're graceful. They have tact. I suppose there's a sinister quality to them, not one I enjoy, but it's something about the grace which makes it possible to tolerate the sinister presence. But it is the great lie about cats, that they lack affection, that they lack character, that they're not interested in anything. If you have them around — particularly if you have more than one — they're an endless source of entertainment. They're very playful and they're very loving, just as loving as dogs. They're all over you — look at the blind one; I mean she's been all over the table, you know, dying to be picked up and to play. You can't call it a sense of humour, but they're also very, very funny. Also, I guess, part of it goes back to a great passage in Stanislavsky about cats and about training for an actor: one of the best things he can do is watch a cat. Because the cat of all living creatures uses its energies most sparingly and with the greatest beauty, in every moment. Have you ever noticed how a cat will drop suddenly and is asleep, or at rest? Cats are a great example of how to use your energy. Beyond that I don't think there's very much to say; I just find them extraordinarily beautiful things to watch, very loving, and just pleasant to have around.

CAMERON: Don't they reveal some conflict in your own mind, in that they're also surely the most overtly hunting of animals?

FINDLEY: No, they aren't. I'm sorry to be so blunt about contradicting you, but I've seen my dogs hunt in tandem and rend a thing apart, which was like a nightmare to me. They killed a raccoon and there was nothing I could do; I got there too late. It was worse than anything I've ever seen in my life. And their joy in doing it was — I've hardly brought myself to forgive them. Except, of course, that you *must* forgive them.

But you see at the same time I believe that—this is going to sound like Saint Francis or something—that what we have as human beings is that marvellous thing of choice, that we may choose not to kill; and if we could get ourselves to that place, we could bring that to the rest of nature, which in essence knows it, to a degree, more than we do. But I grant you that cats are, for instance, one of the animals that kill gratuitously. Most animals don't; most animals kill to eat. I think partly it's their domestication that makes them kill gratuitously. Let's go out and kill something, you know—it almost is like that. They go out and they sit, and there's a great deal of sitting about, looking. But you see, unknown to me, and unliked by me, in myself, I'm sure there is a fascination with violence. And I'm a very violent person myself, inside. I'm sure that I'm more violent in my heart and mind than half the people I criticize for being *overtly* violent, and that makes me hypersensitive to what violence is all about. As a quantity, I live with it day in and day out, whereas the man who resorts to the gun does not. By pulling the trigger, he's exorcised it. That's the awful paradox.

CAMERON: And the cats are like the atmosphere of your novels, almost—they have that very peaceful quality and at the same time that sort of incipient violence.

FINDLEY: I think that's something for you to see, and for me—not to want to see. But you're quite right. Obviously you're quite right. I have no defence against that, except that I'm fighting it, you see. I want them to be different. Crazy? Well, we believe in the rehabilitation of the habitual criminal, and Saint Francis tried a little persuasion on the birds. Me? I have these cats. . . .

CAMERON: All right, that's related to what I'd say if I were asked to describe briefly what your novels are about. They have to do with the qualities of the mind which are private but give rise to public events and actions, the process by which fantasy become action. You get an atmosphere in *The Butterfly Plague* which is almost a psychological equivalent of Nazism, or you get Hooker going through his particular agonies which finally issue in an act. What would you think of such a description?

FINDLEY: I think that's very apt. I think that Hooker has a lot to do with the Kennedy thing and also with the urgency with which we must wipe out the old order. We must destroy what is destroying us. We must kill what is killing us. We must violate the violators, it's all that, and it's a very tough road to walk on, because you're surrounded constantly by the knowledge that what you're asking people to give up is one of the strongest things inside yourself. That's really what I'm doing, as well as some other things, like endings of things. There's always violence, because you hate so strongly what is happening that it can only bring that It Must End sense.

CAMERON: So that you're caught in a contradiction.

FINDLEY: It's a conflict that hopefully will stay entirely inside myself, and that I'll only have to face at the table. The work table, you understand. Do you want some more tea?

June 27, 1971

Timothy Findley:
Biography and Bibliography

Timothy Findley was born in Toronto in 1930. An early interest in ballet developed a taste for performing, and he began acting in summer theatre while supporting himself in a wide variety of temporary jobs. After some time in CBC radio and television drama, he worked at Stratford in its first season before moving to London to attend the Central School of Speech and Drama. Among his professional appearances were The Prisoner *(with Alec Guinness),* The Matchmaker *(with Ruth Gordon), and* Hamlet *(with Paul Scofield). He has written films, and produced a series of film-portraits of theatrical figures including Federico Fellini, Ingmar Bergman, and Kate Reid. In 1962 he gave up acting in favour of full-time writing and broadcasting. He shares an old farmhouse near Cannington, Ontario, with his fellow writer and broadcaster Bill Whitehead.*

Fiction

The Last of the Crazy People (1967)
The Butterfly Plague (1969)

Harold Horwood:

The Senior Freak of Newfoundland

Newfoundland is a very special place; Newfoundlanders are very special people. Harold Horwood—"our Harold", as St. John's Evening Telegram columnist Ray Guy loves to call him—is a very special Newfoundlander. I had sought

Horwood at his home in Beachy Cove, but I had not found him: at the time he was in Fredericton, en route to Toronto, looking for me. We met at last—no doubt inevitably—in Toronto.

According to the calendar, Horwood is middle-aged— and perhaps, if his stocky frame were encased in a suit, he would look fortyish. But he is wearing an open-throated shirt and jeans, bare feet, and his reddish-blond hair sweeps smoothly down over his collar. He has been a longshoreman, a union organizer, a politician, a fighting journalist; now he calls himself a head, a freak, a member of the counter-culture. He speaks clearly, easily, often ironically, and he laughs often. On those bare feet he moves with the grace and controlled energy of a cat, and like a cat he is always alert.

CAMERON: How far is *Tomorrow Will Be Sunday* based on actual historical fact?

HORWOOD: Well, the plot of the book is made up out of whole cloth, so to speak, but the detail, the anecdote as you might describe it, is pretty straight from real life. The incidents that take place in the outport, especially during the first half of the book, are mostly recollections from my father's childhood in Carbonear or my sister-in-law's childhood in another outport. I had never lived in an outport when I wrote *Tomorrow Will Be Sunday*; I visited occasionally, but there's not very much personal experience at all in it. It's part of the word-of-mouth folklore of Newfoundland, these stories. There really *was* a man, for instance, who really did build a little flake on his roof, and cook dumplings and some other things, and take them up there to feed the Lord when He had His Second Advent. There really *was* a case where people went out to the graveyard, and spent the night praying, believing the Lord was coming that night. And so on throughout the whole piece. There really *was* a case where two boys heard an old woman praying for bread and delivered it. There's one bit of personal experience in it. There's an old lady called Aunt Esther, who dies in the course of the book—and this was the first close personal experience I had with death. There was an old lady, a great-aunt of mine, who did die in this way, and it's pretty much a direct description.

CAMERON: The folk culture of Newfoundland seems to provide a lot of the strength that goes into the writing you do.

HORWOOD: In this particular book I set out to write a story that would be interesting in itself, and that would state some of the things I believe about life. But a number of things in it make it a strong book, and this wealth of background detail is one of them. I think I managed to capture the essential nature of Newfoundland outports in the book, and this was indicated to me by the fact that a number of people who live in outports have come to me and said, Look, you must have been writing about Trinity, weren't you? Or, Look, what part of the country were you writing about?—and I discovered that they were thinking about Sound Island in Placentia Bay. People who grew up in every part of Newfoundland firmly believed that I had the particular little town that they grew up in in mind when I wrote about Caplin Bight. The other strength of the book is something that Glenn Gould pointed out to me once, which he called the "celebration of the land". I had never heard the term before—it may be a general one among critics—but I thought about it, and yes, this book does celebrate the land in a very big way. Farley Mowat said once, The thing this book will be remembered for is not the plot, and not what you have to say about it, but the fact that it captures Newfoundland in a way that nothing else ever has. Captures it in an indefinable way of course, whereas in a book like my travel book, *Newfoundland*, I've tried in a direct kind of way to say what Newfoundland is like.

CAMERON: You didn't grow up yourself in an outport, then. Where *did* you grow up?

HORWOOD: I grew up partly in the city and partly just outside the city, but not in an outport. When I was a child I visited

Carbonear occasionally. Carbonear was formerly a big fishing and trading settlement in Conception Bay—population about three thousand; that's big by Newfoundland standards. And I had an aunt living there that I spent some time with occasionally, but just for brief periods. I had nothing to do with fishermen, as I recall, at all, in my childhood. I fished with a fishing crew one summer but this was after I'd become a man and a journalist, in fact.

CAMERON: How did you become a journalist—or a novelist?

HORWOOD: Well, I think you're born with genius or not, you know, at least born with the potentiality. But what you do with it depends on your character. For every writer who does something with himself as a writer, there must be a hundred with just as much talent, just as much inherent ability, perhaps even more inherent ability, who, for one reason or another, never become writers, or become writers and cease to be writers very quickly. There's some indefinable thing, you know, the stiffness of the backbone, the stubbornness and the faith in yourself, the general ego and all this kind of thing. My brother and I were both writing, both publishing a little magazine called *Protocol* back in the 1940s and he was far better than I was. But he ceased to be a writer altogether and became an accountant. I might have ceased to be a writer and become a politician; Joe Smallwood almost tempted me into this. If Smallwood had been less repellent as a person, when you got to know him— well, this is not fair, he's not repellent. But if his politics had been a little more democratic I might have wound up as a politician.

CAMERON: A politician? Look, you'd better go back to the beginning.

HORWOOD: I went to school in Newfoundland, and then I got into the labour movement and into—not free-lance writing —into avant-garde publishing I guess you'd have to call it, at the same time. We began publishing a literary magazine and at the same time we were working as longshoremen on the waterfront—this is my brother and myself back in the 1940s.

I went from that into various sorts of casual labour; I worked as a rodman for surveying crews, as a checker on construction jobs, I worked in a garage — I was a grease-monkey — I worked as a carpenter's helper on construction work. I got into the labour movement through politics, I guess. There was a Labour Party organized in Newfoundland, and I was a socialist by conviction. Some of the labour leaders came to me and said, Look, we want you to help us out with this thing. So they made me campaign manager for their first election there, and through being a campaign manager for the Labour Party I got into the labour movement as such, and became a labour organizer. This is sort of back-assed, the opposite to the way it usually happens, but this is the way it happened with me. And then for a few years I was a full-time labour organizer and head of the biggest union in St. John's for a while — the first successful industrial-type union.

Then Joe Smallwood picked me up from the labour movement, because he assumed I was a person who could influence votes, and said, Look, we're going to organize a campaign to get Newfoundland into Confederation; I think you should join in and give us a hand. I did, not ever intending to go into politics. I'd started out intending only to work with the Confederation campaign and once that was accomplished then to go back into private life. But again, he talked me into running for a district in 1949, so I was member for Labrador for the first term. At the end of the term, which only lasted two years, when he called the second election I decided I didn't want to go back, and that ended my association with him. I spent the first two months after I got out of politics organizing the Division of Northern Labrador Services. The government took over from the Hudson's Bay Company in Labrador and we organized the Division on the basis of being not just a trading operation, but a welfare operation which included trading at a deliberate loss. I wasn't paid for it or anything, it was just something I did as a service to the district I had been representing. When that was completed, everybody expected that

I was going to be appointed director of this government division. It was the obvious thing: a guy who's just left the government builds up and organizes a new division of the civil service, and naturally he becomes the head of it. But I decided I didn't want to be the head of it and I selected another man.

Then I was left not knowing what I was going to do, so I said everything I've done has been a matter of training myself to be a writer; the next step is to go into journalism. I went to the *Evening Telegram* in St. John's and said, I want to become a journalist. And Jim Herder, who was the head of the paper, said, Well... you mean really a career as a journalist, do you? not just a few months or something? I said, No, I mean a career; I'll guarantee to stay at least two years. So they gave me a job as political reporter reporting the House of Assembly, the obvious thing, and they subsequently sent me to Ottawa to the National Press Gallery for a while. Then I became a columnist and subsequently editor of the editorial page, with the title of Associate Editor, and I also edited the news page for a while. In fact, I think I could say I did every job on the newspaper except advertising. But early in '58 I felt myself getting stale. I'd been six years on the newspaper and I was as far as you could get; there were no further promotions possible. I'd been writing a political column that just about set everybody on their ear. We—I and the paper—were sued repeatedly for libel by members of the government. During that period it was the principal voice of opposition to Smallwood in Newfoundland—you might say it was the *only* voice. The opposition in the House of Assembly, in so far as it was effective at all, took its effectiveness from me; I gave them virtually all the material that they used. It was a fighting, campaigning, crusading column—an opposition column. The paper had real backbone; they could not be intimidated by the government, no matter what. They would have let the place be locked up before they'd bow down and say, We'll publish what you tell us to, and not publish what you won't. In all the various libel suits there was never any question of settlement or compromise. We were being sued for a million dollars at one time, which was a lot of money in the 1950s.

But by 1958 it was getting pretty stale and I was tired of the whole thing. Farley Mowat had been shuttling back and forth to Newfoundland for a couple of years and he and I had been bombing around the province in a car; that particular year he phoned me from the mainland and said, I'm arriving at Stephenville, could you meet me there at the airport? So I drove across the island and picked him up and we went on another one of our drunken tours of the outports. We wound up at St. John's and at this point I simply walked into the office and said, Look, I'm supposed to be coming back from my holidays now; I'm sorry, I can't do it, I've got to leave, even though it's without notice. And I went to the treasurer and said, Please cash the bonds I hold in the company. I'm just going to take them and get out. He said, I suppose there's nothing in the way of a raise in salary or anything that would interest you? and I said, No. I was so deeply involved in the paper that if I had gone through the normal processes I could never have torn myself away from it at all.

So at that point I just got out and started free-lance writing. It was what I expected—my income fell to almost zero for a couple of years and then gradually I picked up, bit by bit, you know. I sold an article to *Maclean's*, and sold an article to *Star Weekly*, and sold an article to *Weekend*, the markets that pay reasonably well. Then CBC began using bits and pieces of my stuff, and eventually when CBC television began trying to be Canadian instead of just Toronto, they started looking for the occasional writer from some other part of the country. It was funny: they approached me and said, We want you to do a television script. I said, I've never written a script of any kind, I have no idea how scripts are written. And they said, Well, we can probably supply you with one—and they dug up a script by Frank Willis and sent it down to me. It had all kinds of stuff about camera angles and everything, so I wrote a script with all this stuff in it and they accepted it. And for the next few years I was in constant demand. That tided me over until my first novel was published, *Tomorrow Will Be Sunday*. Fortunately it made me some money, and fortunately I had another book waiting to go soon afterwards.

CAMERON: *The Foxes of Beachy Cove?*

HORWOOD: Right. Both these books, while they weren't run-away best-sellers or anything, earned me enough to live on for a year, what with the advance and the subsequent royalties. If *Tomorrow Will Be Sunday* had flopped, I might never have been able to go on, because I might have been forced financially to go back to full-time journalism.

CAMERON: At one time you did a socialist newspaper, too, didn't you?

HORWOOD: Oh yes. After I got out of the *Telegram* in 1958, the I.W.A. strike took place in Newfoundland and some really terrible things happened. This was when Smallwood showed his true colours as a real strike-breaker. I got involved as a public relations officer, writing press releases and things of this sort for the Newfoundland Federation of Labour, especially during the I.W.A. strike. Then after the strike had been lost they decided they wanted to publish a weekly newspaper, directed toward the labour movement. So Ed Finn, who had resigned as managing editor of the *Western Star* in Corner Brook because of the newspaper's policy during the strike, and myself, agreed to publish a newspaper. The paper was labour-oriented and socialist, the first paper in Canada that officially backed what was then called the New Party, before they had added the word Democratic to it. We published it for almost a year, but we discontinued it voluntarily, because we could foresee that the paper was going to get into financial trouble.

CAMERON: What do you think of my thesis that you really can't do serious journalism in this day and age, because you won't even notice the issues, unless you in some way profoundly dissent from the way the society wags?

HORWOOD: I don't think anybody is worth a damn in any field of endeavour unless he profoundly dissents. We're living in a society in which the Establishment, which includes all the people who control the society, is still nineteenth-century and they're still thinking in nineteenth-century terms. And unless you dissent from this, you're nowhere. It doesn't matter what you're into, in your art, in literature, in teaching, in any field. It's a very sad fact that the only possible hope of rescuing North American society from a total state of decadence and stagnation is the success of the revolution. I suppose too that artists have always been revolutionaries. The artist has always been the dirty-water walker—the fellow that is hated and outcast and despised by society. And it's so now, same as it always was. It's nonsense to think that we're basically any different. The people who get idolized now are the pseudo types, not the real ones. The real people who are doing the real things are the ones who go to jail for it. Just as they did in previous generations.

CAMERON: That belief shows in your work.

HORWOOD: Certainly. In my next novel, *The Toslow Fire Sutra*, which I'm publishing in 1973, I have tried to translate into a novel the true experience of the current generation, the real experience of the revolution that goes on in your soul rather than outside, the real experience of the counter-culture. And the drug experience, the acid trip, the profound experience of vision—not in bits and pieces, but as an integrated whole. I haven't done it as a reporter, from the outside, but as a person deeply involved, a person who's been there. And I *have* been there, you see; I actually joined the counter-culture, several years past. I think to really write effectively about anything, you have to be there.

CAMERON: What determined you to join the counter-culture?

HORWOOD: Oh, my nephew dragged me into it by the heels. I have a house at Beachy Cove which has always been sort of open to anybody who wanted to open the door and come in, and John, after he turned on to rock music during his last year of high school, began bringing his friends in there and playing the Fugs, and the Doors, and the Mothers of Invention on the record player. I think he set out deliberately to convert me, suspecting that I might be the only person of my generation in Newfoundland who might be *capable* of being converted. He's never said this, but I really think he must have made a conscious effort to do it, because all of a sudden I found myself wrapped up very deeply in it indeed — you know, suddenly I could *hear* rock music and I could understand the way these people were thinking and began thinking the way they did. All the ethics, all the values of the square society that I had always been in sort of unconscious revolt against — all of a sudden the whole thing crystallized. You don't just stay there and fight it from the inside. You get out. This theory that you continually hear from square people, that the only way you can effectively oppose something is to be part of it, is the most specious nonsense. You can't oppose anything at all if you're part of it. You get out and you go your way — quietly or violently, depending on your particular type of personality. You either oppose things the way Thoreau opposed them, or you oppose them the way Eldridge Cleaver opposes them, but in either case you have to get outside the thing and oppose it from the outside.

CAMERON: Is opposition the main point of the counter-culture for you?

HORWOOD: Oh no, the counter-culture has a lot of facets to it — everything from brown rice to new styles in art and poetry. For instance, the book of poetry that I'm putting together now was written by four — two very young and two somewhat older — members of the counter-culture in Newfoundland. It's a book of refreshing simplicity — you know, you don't *have to* have some American post-graduate English critic go through it word by word and explain what it means to you. Anybody can understand it and this is the way writing should be. Same thing with art. The art that's being done now by the new artists is not a lot of private, indecipherable design; it isn't something that just exists in the mind of the creator; it's something that the viewer can look at and see and make some sense of, even if he doesn't get all the depth of it at first sight. Same thing with the poetry: this poetry is quite simple at first reading, you're not just stymied by the stuff. It has, of course, various levels of subtlety in it, so you may have to read it several times. Visual art is getting into this sort of basic simplicity too, out of the quagmire that both writing and art were in the 1940s and '50s and to some extent in the '60s.

CAMERON: You're expressing a radicalism in the grain which astonished me in *Tomorrow Will Be Sunday*. As you say, you may very well be the only person in your generation in Newfoundland who could have been converted to the counter-culture.

HORWOOD: Well, at that point I wasn't.

CAMERON: No, but a man who could write that novel obviously *could* be.

HORWOOD: Yes, that's right. And Chris is dead, but Eli becomes the protagonist of *The Toslow Fire Sutra*. A lot of people wondered what happened to Eli after the end of *Tomorrow Will Be Sunday*. Originally I had sort of a postscript written to it, and he had become just a drifter, which is exactly what I would have thought Eli might have become under the circumstances. But Jack McClelland said, My God, no! You can't have this, you'll have to cut it out — Jack gave me some advice on the book, although he didn't eventually publish it. I did cut it out and I just threw it away — but Eli became a freak, which is exactly what he should have become, after having become various other things first. The possibility of it is there, all right. I wasn't Eli in *Tomorrow Will Be Sunday*, but I'm Eli in *The Toslow Fire Sutra*. Between the two novels Eli has become me.

CAMERON: Maybe it's just that I don't understand Newfoundland, but I see you as something of a sport in that society.

HORWOOD: I think you get more radicalism in Newfoundland than in any of the other Atlantic provinces. There's a larger number of "heads" per thousand around St. John's than any other city in the Maritimes unless you include Truro as a city; although Truro is a small town, they may have a larger "head" population — at least they did a couple of years ago. But Halifax, for instance, is a conservative town compared to St. John's.

St. John's has always been radical in many ways: the direct contact with Europe, the fact that St. John's people sailed all over the world. This was the way of life, the real profession of the port, international trade; it wasn't fishing. And there's been a tradition of political radicalism on the island, a very, very strong tradition. There were several attempts at revolution, you know; the Newfoundland Regiment was disbanded by the British government at one time for mutiny. The Irish attempted to take over the government at one stage, a real insurrection. And you had Coaker with the first successful primary producers' union ever organized in North America. It went on to get within an ace of capturing the government. They were organized first in 1910, but by 1913 this fishermen's union, organized on what was then the most radical lines, held the balance of power in the legislature. If they hadn't had certain basic structural faults from the beginning, they would have taken over the government and Great Britain would have had to send in the marines to kick them out of power as they did in other colonies when radical governments came into power. There would have been a revolutionary socialist government in power in Newfoundland at the time of the First World War, if Coaker had really known what he was doing. He was not a very well-read man; he didn't know much about the history of radical movements. He just sort of dreamt the thing up himself. But he had forty thousand people in that union at one time.

CAMERON: What about your own family? Is there a strong dissenting tradition in it?

HORWOOD: Dissent in the sense of religious dissent. My father's family had been Methodists, I guess, and his branch of the family embraced the Salvation Army, which was a sort of religious radicalism. Then he went from that into various more radical fundamentalist or self-fundamentalist groups. A friend of mine once suggested to me that the Protestant habit of forming ever smaller splinter groups, and of questioning the religious establishment, was one of the great bases for all political radicalism. My grandfather was a dissenter too, in other ways, not religiously because he never had much religious conviction one way or the other, but he was a foreign-going captain and he rebelled against the conventions, you know. He refused to prosecute the seal fishery. He went once, and would never go again, even though this was back at the turn of the century, because he regarded the killing of baby seals as too barbarous a thing for a civilized man to engage in. He lost his ticket for taking a ship away from a pilot that he believed was likely to wreck the ship because the pilot was drunk. There's a very strong tradition of people being individuals, being themselves rather than part of an organization.

CAMERON: Did your father's experience have something to do with your grasp of Brother John and his whole religious outlook?

HORWOOD: This is difficult — my father has never belonged to this sort of mad religion that expected the Lord to come again next week or the week after or something. The people in Newfoundland who are into this trip are the Pentecostal Church and a few others of that type. There are some even smaller sects, one called the Saints Gathered Together in the Name of the Lord Jesus, and these were the people I was thinking of when I wrote the book. My father's youth and village undoubtedly added some colour to it, but he would be the last person to associate himself with Brother John. This sort of wild-eyed fundamentalism was completely anathema to him.

CAMERON: Could somebody like Chris have survived in that outport? And wouldn't somebody like Eli be most unlikely to have taken on Chris's attitude in the face of the social pressure against it?

HORWOOD: No, I don't think it's unlikely at all. I think that the book is highly probable the way it is, because, you see, in the latter part of the novel I attempted to explain the basically civilized attitudes of the fishermen, of the Newfoundlander — you know, they take up with these wild religious movements but subconsciously they aren't this way, and when something happens they tend to go back to the more civilized thing. When Chris came back to the settlement he was immediately accepted, and this is exactly the way it would have been in a Newfoundland outport. Newfoundland fishermen are really tolerant people. For instance, the long-haired hippies have no problem at all in the outports. Free-lance journalists, guys with hair down to the shoulders and bare feet, have gone into the outports. Someone in St. John's would just look at one of these guys and say, He wants to live in an *outport*? He must be out of his mind, no one is even going to talk to him. But one of these fellows has done this, he's gone; he specialized in the outports and he made a lot of close friends among the fishermen, and he has now become an organizer for the new fishermen's union which is being organized at the present time — I mean, a real outright hippie, and the fishermen have accepted him as a union organizer. There's this kind of tolerance among the fishermen which you don't get among the city people. A lot of the young people have gone out to the outports, have gotten taken on as sharesmen in fishing crews and things like that without any difficulty at all.

CAMERON: You've been through a lot of changes.

HORWOOD: It's the tragedy of so many writers, that many of them cease to change. They become fossilized, and they spend their lives mining whatever lode they discovered in their youth. This certainly isn't the kind of writer that I am, or I wouldn't be involved with the turned-on generation right now as deeply as I am — as a member of it, as a freak if you like. In your youth you go through periods of being torn apart inside, but if you're lucky you resolve your internal conflicts, most of them. The only serious conflict in me at the moment is the conflict between work and the ability to do it. I work much more slowly than I ought to and I've got the feeling that I'm terribly lazy.

CAMERON: More so than you used to be?

HORWOOD: No, I don't think so. I think all the serious work

I've ever done has been done very slowly. It took me five years to write *Tomorrow Will Be Sunday*. The basic work that went into *The Foxes of Beachy Cove* was going on for a couple of years, I suppose, based on things I'd been doing, but the writing of the book only occupied six or seven weeks. *Newfoundland* again was a book based on a lot of journalism that I'd done, so I simply had to pull out drawers, either in my mind or in a filing cabinet. I wrote that book complete, including all revisions and the index and all the rest of it, in five weeks. So I wouldn't say the pace has been slowing down. The novel that's now ready to be published, *The Toslow Fire Sutra*, I started in November 1969, and that winter I was involved in Animal Farm° and working part-time at the newspaper, so I didn't really have much time. But I still finished it in about fourteen months or something. The other book, the Labrador novel, *White Eskimo*, is something that I've been fooling around with, in the way of making notes and stuff, for a number of years.

CAMERON: Tell me about that book.

HORWOOD: This is a more traditional type of novel. *White Eskimo* doesn't have the radical structure of *The Toslow Fire Sutra*; it's a traditionally structured novel. I don't have a lot of flashbacks, I'm not monkeying around with the chronologies, and I'm not having things happening in people's minds. It's written as *Tomorrow Will Be Sunday* was, in a completely chronological, third-person way, where you see the story through the eyes of a single character, who is there and who tells it in a straightforward manner. The book is consciously into the mythological in the sense that it goes back to the old hero epic. The epic actually relates the mythological material to recent life in the days of the fur trade in Labrador. It incidentally recounts the social history of Labrador, but this simply comes in as background. And it's a deliberate revolt against the anti-hero. Gillingham is a *real* hero. A person who is worth

°An astonishing free school in St. John's. See Horwood's own account of it in *The Mysterious East*, March/April 1971.

writing about needs to be an extraordinary person, someone larger than life.

CAMERON: You don't mind fostering the idea that there *are* people larger than life?

HORWOOD: Well, there *are*, you meet 'em all the time. Joe Smallwood's larger than life, in his own miserable way. Trudeau is larger than life. He's the type of whom legends are made, as Macdonald was. This fur-trader revolutionary who lived in Labrador at this particular time has become a legend; he *had* to have the qualities that make legends, and he *was* larger than life in many respects. I can see authors being worried by it, I can very well see it. I can see them being sort of afraid of it, too. But one of the things you have to do too is follow your own convictions whether other people believe in them or not, and I think you have to dare to do the things that you want to do. You know, if I happen to believe in heroes, and I happen to like them, and I happen to dislike anti-heroes, and I happen to believe in personalities and so on, well, even if this is an era in which these things are not accepted, then I have to go ahead with them anyway. Even dare to be old-fashioned.

CAMERON: You say *White Eskimo* is consciously mythological. A lot of Canadian writers seem to be fascinated by myth these days.

HORWOOD: I think every person has a mythological background in himself and often a mythological background in his work whether he appreciates it or not. *Tomorrow Will Be Sunday*, for instance, is based on the myth of the New Testament. The names—Eli and Christopher, etc.—are not accidents. Christopher is a Christ figure in a mild sort of way, and so on. There's a sort of mythological structure to any story. The attitudes, the things you accept as being basically true, all form a body of myth of one sort or another.

CAMERON: I was in Newfoundland recently, and I almost think the whole province a mythological community.

HORWOOD: Well, it's a small nation. Newfoundland nationalism is a completely natural thing—nothing artificial about it.

It hasn't been fostered, it isn't something that somebody is trying to create, it's just there. Because we *were* a separate nation for three hundred and fifty or four hundred years, small as we were—and during this time we became a distinct people. There's a distinct ethos in Newfoundland, and it's still there, and will be for a long time to come, I'd say. You don't even have to talk about it; it just *is* a little nation of its own.

June 27, 1971

Harold Horwood:
Biography and Bibliography

Harold Horwood was born at St. John's, Newfoundland, in 1923, into a family of writers. His grandfather, Captain John Horwood, published numerous historical articles. His father, Andrew Horwood, has published one book, Newfoundland Ships and Men, *and a chapbook of poetry. His brother, Charles, has published a book of lyrics. After frolicking through enough careers to satisfy a platoon of mere mortals— longshoring, labouring, avant-garde publishing, politics, union organizing, newspapering—he became a free-lance writer in 1962. In normal circumstances (which occur rarely) he lives at Beachy Cove, outside St. John's.*

Fiction

Tomorrow Will Be Sunday (1966)
White Eskimo (1972)

Non-Fiction

The Foxes of Beachy Cove (1967)
Newfoundland (1969)
(editor) *Voices Underground* (1972)

Robert Kroetsch:

The American Experience
and the Canadian Voice

*Robert Kroetsch's brawling and lusty novels are set in Alberta
and along the Mackenzie River, and they speak of a world of
pork-barrel politics, horse-breeding, Bible-pounders, and
river boatmen. Kroetsch himself is discovered in the decaying*

industrial city of Binghamton, in upstate New York, where he teaches English at the local branch of the State University. At forty-four, Kroetsch is brown-haired, with a thick brown moustache; he drives a white Pontiac sedan and lives in a pleasant home on a shady side street. But we decide to talk at his office, which will be quieter.

Kroetsch is shy and soft-spoken; he speaks slowly, with long pauses sprinkled through his talk. He is candid, modest, and often droll, and each of us seems to trigger ideas in the other, so that two hours pass before we break for coffee in the student cafeteria, and another hour or more flips by before we call it a day and go for steamed clams and beer at a workingman's tavern downtown. Leaving Binghamton in the warm May twilight, I realize that I have not just conducted an interview: I have found a friend.

CAMERON: You said in a conversation with Margaret Laurence that you were working on a trilogy.

KROETSCH: That's what I have in mind. *The Words of My Roaring* is the first volume, set in the thirties. *The Studhorse Man* takes place at the end of the war. The third is to be, in its own peculiar way, contemporary. Right now I'd call it *Funeral Games*.

CAMERON: In the published section of *Funeral Games*, there's a kind of Kafkaesque quality which you seem to be giving more and more rein to.

KROETSCH: In a way that's true. I'm fascinated right now by the effects of moving away from realism — the kinds of freedom you get, and the kinds of truth you get at, by departing from the sterner varieties of realism. I'm not so sure anyone has a "realistic" experience; it's a literary convention to begin with, the notion of realism. We get a false sense of communion out of that convention. We all see the Administration Building when we land at the Edmonton Airport, but beyond that what distinctions are operating? Each traveller has his own subjective response to the experience of travel, his own anxieties, his own sense of the significance of colour and space — and space fascinates me right now. I'm taking a character out of the city and into a new sense of space and having him confront it. I'm interested in the easterner going west, the city boy going out to that kind of space.

CAMERON: I take it he's a native American. Do you have difficulty getting inside the mind of an American?

KROETSCH: Well, I guess I don't really think of him so much as an American — but rather as a man whose childhood was spent in a huge American city. I don't trust those larger generalizations, though I recognize we can't avoid them. All over the world people are moving from the country into the city. But the American Dream goes the other way. So I take a character who grew up in Greenwich Village and watch him confronting his own vision of the northwest — and I think I understand that. The American view of Canada has changed so radically, remoulding Canada as part of, as a corrective to, the failing dream. Young Americans are seeing in Canada right now — and they come to my office to ask questions but give me the answers — the sense of space, the sense of freedom, the sense of authentic experience, even, that they believe they can no longer get here in the east. But I want to follow through and see what happens when the dreamer really goes and makes his visit.

CAMERON: You went the other direction yourself.

KROETSCH: Yes. I think in my coming to the United States I discovered how hopelessly Canadian I am, in my sense of what reality is. There are some Canadians who come here and very quickly out-American the Americans in their assimilation of this culture. I feel more separate from it now than I did ten years ago. Perhaps I understand it better, but the past ten years haven't exactly made America lovable. I really want to come to terms with my sense of this American-Canadian thing more clearly. I find that I'm going to write something about it. I've always rather disliked Henry James' novels, but I imagine one day in his life he must have recognized that he had experienced two cultures in a way that was significant — and that's just how I feel. Almost by accident, I've had this double experience, and I've got to write it out. In a comic way, perhaps; not in any sociological way.

CAMERON: Why does the world present itself to you in comic terms?

KROETSCH: Well, at one time I was very much into the theory of comedy, reading Frye and all those cats. It's very difficult to talk about. Like life, it's bigger than theory. I suppose Canadians have a front-row seat on power and yet feel powerless quite often, and develop a sense of the absurd out of their own predicament. Like the great Canadian passion to buy life insurance, in the face — No, that's not what I mean. Living here — even as you watch the sequence of American elections, you develop a sense of irony, of *déjà vu*. They seem so desperately serious about it; yet in their "free elections" there isn't any way to vote for anything that would make even slight alterations in the existing system. But the Americans involved manage to be innocent each time the election ritual begins. I think we've got a sense of memory that's different from theirs, and maybe again a sense of futility, I don't know. The Canadian sense of history is something that needs much exploring — but it must be unique. We can ignore history completely and with ease, and yet we can be overwhelmed by history at opportune moments. It's a strange combination.

CAMERON: What do you mean by ignoring history?

KROETSCH: Perhaps I speak as a westerner. In the rhetoric of prairie politics — in the voices of Riel, Tommy Douglas, Aberhart, Diefenbaker — we go from Eden to the apocalypse in one easy leap. They never quite know whether it's the end or the beginning. I was playing with it a little bit in *The Words of My Roaring*. There's very little credence given to the notion that we exist in history, in time.

CAMERON: You don't see this in the States, then?

KROETSCH: In the United States, the Freudian metaphor has swept the boards, the superego versus the id kind of thing. The id is the good guy trying to free himself, and the superego takes many forms, the government, or the military-industrial complex, or, in recent history, the universities. The good guy is the youth or the frontiersman, the man in the ten-gallon hat. I see in Canada much less excitement about that particular Freudian metaphor. I suspect we're more Jungian in some way. We see opposites in necessary balance all the time—maybe that becomes paralysing, I don't know. If you accept the Freudian view there's lots of room for will. Either you're clamping down or you're freeing yourself. But we're caught in a balance, and not only the French-English one, though that's the supreme political one. The hope-despair balance is fascinating to me, because that's the razor's edge; that's where we live. We become fascinated with problems of equilibrium. Americans are interested in expansion. This difference has to have an effect on our literature, on our language.

CAMERON: You once said we speak a new language in Canada.

KROETSCH: I would guess that we have to, to accommodate to our own convictions. Yes, I see it reflected in our writers. Hugh Hood. Rudy Wiebe. Buckler. I suppose it's regional, a little bit. Perhaps there's a bit more flamboyance in the west, something inside the form that threatens it. The urban Ontario voice is the victory of form over feeling. Then, a voice that I admire, even envy, is the Maritime voice—which you know more about than I do. It's a tremendously rich language they speak there: the oral tradition which is the stuff of literature. It's like the prairies: people talk about each other, not about what they saw on television or read about in the newspapers. It's virtually oral, and that's where writers find liberation. What we have to do in Canada is concentrate on hearing this voice that is within us, and trusting it. In Toronto they love to hire English TV and radio people, because we don't trust this

Canadian voice. When we hear ourselves, we're not quite sure what we're hearing.

CAMERON: In going back through *But We Are Exiles* the other day I especially noticed the Newfoundland speech.

KROETSCH: In my years in the north country I had the good fortune to work with a number of Newfoundlanders. I couldn't begin to write a first-person novel with a Newfoundlander speaking. But what a yarn that would be! You know, American writers in the nineteenth century had a choice between their own voices and a literary voice, with Longfellow electing to work within the convention, while Whitman dared to sing himself. I see Canadian writers facing the same choice. There are very tempting other voices around us. The American voice is one of them, and it may be the most obvious temptation. It has authority, it has directness, it has confidence. But Canadians still have to elect for this relatively unknown voice that is theirs, and make literature out of that. And a difficult task it is; because "ordinary speech" is a convention-bound language, and yet the language of prose...

CAMERON: Do you find it an exhilarating experience writing and working with that voice?

KROETSCH: Yes, I do, because I guess I'm a frontiersman and I like the sense of its newness. I suppose that for an English writer it must be very satisfying to think you're using a language that's been a literary language for hundreds of years; but for us, at least our generation of Canadian writers, it's the very opposite experience. It's the excitement of having something that's brand new, just as Twain may have felt it in the United States.

CAMERON: Right, Twain would be the American analogue. Which brings us back to humour.

KROETSCH: Sure, Twain finally makes a literary form out of the things that had been accumulating behind him — comedy, the use of the frontier, all those terrible books written in dialect. He suddenly got hold of that raw material and made it work.

CAMERON: Maybe there's a relation between the new voice and the humour. Since you can't trust people to take the voice seriously, you authenticate it by pushing it over into comedy.

KROETSCH: That may be right. You clown a little bit. Certainly Twain did that, except of course underneath his clowning was a terribly bitter streak.

CAMERON: Right—the clowning conveys something quite serious. The macabre streak in your work is really the opposite side of your humour, isn't it? The humour pulls you in and then the other things that are going on underneath make themselves apparent.

KROETSCH: You're onto something, yes. Twain was working with a language that hadn't quite been recognized as a serious literary language. And so he clowns, and maybe he clowns too much, even, at times in some of his minor works, as if he's not sure himself that he can bring it off as a literary language. But at his best he's magnificent.

CAMERON: Like that lovely scene in which Hazard with his milk-wagon gets into the swearing match with the truck driver. That's like a tall tale.

KROETSCH: Oh sure, exactly. It *is* part of the tall tale tradition. You see this in beer parlours in the west: the delight in insulting and verbal quarrelling, where people tend to make each other larger than life. But behind that there is a very serious movement toward, a need for, myth-making.

CAMERON: Now in *The Studhorse Man* the narrator becomes much more important than in the previous two—and he does a kind of mad parody of scholarship—

KROETSCH: —Right.

CAMERON: In that novel, aren't you taking a character who is potentially mythological, and treating him with the utmost seriousness, in a scholarly way—but that's not quite legitimate, with somebody like that, and so you make that scholar just a little daft?

KROETSCH: Yeah. I'm doing a parody of biography, because if you think about undertaking to capture another man's life, that's a pretty fantastic notion — and yet you do capture something. So it's working both ways, in the parody and in the sharp contrast between the two men, the one completely static, the other the roving dream figure. But yes, Proudfoot finally tells us something. It's that nice balance that I'm interested in.

CAMERON: And he tells us progressively more about himself, too.

KROETSCH: Sure, because in writing biography, when you're telling another man's story, you have to be involved yourself. This "scholar" is not quite good enough to keep himself in rein, and slowly he takes over. It has other implications, too: how we relate to a story, to characters. At what point do they become us? When do we derive a self from these other selves?

CAMERON: You mention the static figure and the roving figure. But that book was full of other oppositions, too.

KROETSCH: Well, it's a dialectic of sorts. We get the choices we face in life, between stasis and motion, between thought and action, between — well, I had others in mind, as I recall. Even the flesh and the spirit.

CAMERON: And between the morality which comes from the free play of impulse and the morality which comes from the careful —

KROETSCH: That's right: control and chaos, or morality and liberation from that, periodically. Some readers said to me: Here's a nice story about this studhorse man, but why did you put that narrator in? One critic read it as straight biography, so he missed the whole thing.

CAMERON: As I look through the three novels, it seems to me I see more and more complexity, and it's related to that question of tone.

KROETSCH: I think you're right. That's why Proudfoot, sitting there in his dry bathtub, immobilized, hearing his own voice and talking about this pattern of action — he intrigues me. But what is tone? Ultimately tone reveals how you feel about what you're saying; you gamble that your reader's going to *hear* some of it. It's a huge gamble in that if the reader doesn't hear

Proudfoot's voice, it's going to be a very different novel. He's got to hear the edges all the time; and that puts him to work, judging.

CAMERON: So are your experiments almost all linguistic?

KROETSCH: I like to think I'm doing some new things with the trilogy itself, as a form. But yes, in writing a novel I have to wait until I myself begin to hear the voice — the voice that at first is too distant, but then starts to usurp my own. I had that trouble with *The Words*: I was giving lectures in the voice of Johnnie Backstrom. In this trilogy I'm trying three different voices which together add up — maybe to a fourth. I don't know. You pay a high price for using first person, for getting at that awareness of subjectivity.

CAMERON: You work pretty well exclusively in first person.

KROETSCH: So far I have. I like to feel that someday I might again use third person validly. The misuse of third person is so easy. It's become very difficult to use third person well. It leads to an easy kind of characterization. You can step outside and give a summary, instead of dramatizing what the character is. It leads to reader manipulation, where the author tells the reader how to respond without earning the reader's response: and then it leads to an easy use of a borrowed language, a kind of literary third-person voice which is not too hard to pick up.

CAMERON: Does third person depend on the shared experience, the common view?

KROETSCH: That's exactly it, that's exactly it. We're reduced to private visions in our time — there's no longer a trust in the shared, the community vision. The change from third person to first person implies a change in our view of what we know and how we know it.

CAMERON: You've said that in *The Studhorse Man* the trickster figure is the penis. Is that another one of our oppositions, knowledge and innocence, virginity and experience?

KROETSCH: The trickster — he's the force that gets you out of the rational frame. Out of the frame-up. He kicks loose. The modern fascination with the trickster figure simply indicates the degree to which we find our present society oppressive. The tedium of conformity drives us into fantasies of escape. Proudfoot is quite literally under lock and key; but no one can stop him from associating himself with Hazard Lepage, not even the shrinks. Perhaps it was Rodin who said that ultimately the trickster is comparable with the penis: they're both irrational, unpredictable. They do their own things.

CAMERON: What about the relationship between humans and horses?

KROETSCH: Well—

CAMERON: Well, why do you have this sexual obsession with horses?

KROETSCH: To dodge your question, the horse along with the bull is the most universal animal-become-symbol that I can think of. You could—quite comfortably—spend the rest of your life studying the significance of the horse in art and literature. It's got power, it's beautiful, it's creative, it's dangerous. It represents the unconscious in certain ways, because of its relationship to freedom. Man and the horse have a long and peculiar relationship of interdependence, as Don Quixote would remind us.

CAMERON: You're tremendously interested in the domestication of Western myth—Western in both senses.

KROETSCH: Yes. Western man—in both senses—is vitally interested in the particularity of his experience and the way it relates to the general, to other people's experience. And one way of talking about that is through myth and story. It's a kind of shorthand for our saying to each other, "I know what you're talking about." After all, why do we read? Partly to share and partly to see something new; that's the novel, the very word itself—novel.

CAMERON: And maybe also to find that the things which seem to us tangible, particular, or individual and new also participate in that kind of common experience which isn't even solely of our time.

KROETSCH: You have to have both dimensions in your life, it seems to me. If you create a society where communal experience is all, the individual gets wiped out. And yet if you simply cultivate the self — well, maybe some of the kids on drugs are trying to do this. I teach creative writing and many of the students are into drugs. A few years ago the drug experience was leading them to a sense of community. In the stuff I've read this year, the drug experience is one of terrible isolation, the self all by itself. Now where is this problem being examined, worked out? I would say — in fiction. Because in fiction you have a big enough canvas, you have room to take a group of characters, a community in effect, through time. While working out the implications of life in a particular place as well as in time. One of the reasons why Canada looks like a good place to live at the moment is just this: it seems, to many Americans, to have struck a more valid balance between the self and the group. You take a thing like the draft: you know, when you teach these eighteen-year-olds and get a sense of what they feel about it, it's not the danger of being killed in Viet Nam. It's what it's doing to the self — a kind of being annihilated. It's no secret that the army has set out to annihilate the sense of individuality, because they have to make you operate in this other construct. And the students feel the universities are interchangeable, and churn out interchangeable people to work for interchangeable corporations any place on earth. The literature of the past can put the same kind of pressure on a writer. Much as I admire *The Odyssey*, I want to get free of it. I want to get loose, and to do it I re-tell the story, I re-enact it, in my own way.

CAMERON: Your novels read very easily, very lightly, but actually you're dealing with images which are rather macabre. *But We Are Exiles* opens with dragging for a body, and two of your novels wind up with the catastrophic death of the hero. You write about undertakers and body robbing. It's not quite a preoccupation with death; it's a preoccupation with corpses.

KROETSCH: Canadian life is so much a daylight world if you stop and think about it. So much of our prose — and maybe poetry too, I would say — is the stuff of daylight. And yet there is an underworld, a night-time to Canadian life, and I'm fascinated by that night-time. American literature is very much a night literature: they're fascinated by their underground journeys, their Moby Dicks, their Hawthornes. Canadians so often gloss that over with a nice sparkly surface. So that's what I aimed at, not a sparkly surface, but what would look like a simple, *reliable* surface, and I worked hard at getting that surface to carry the light.

Then you begin to suspect what lies beneath it. I want to have both those things operating, both that clinging to day that we have, and yet that awareness of a tremendous undertow, the night, the night journey, or whatever. In contemporary American writing, there's too easy a descent into the night world. You want to say to them, now wait a minute: there's twenty-four hours in a day and I know that you're involved around the clock. I hope the thrust of Canadian writing will be to keep that tension in mind, as Peggy Atwood does so successfully. I don't trust the Canadian impulse to dwell only in daylight. But to see only night, as so many New York writers seem to do — that's easy too. It's wrong. In *But We Are Exiles* you have the literal surface of the water as your dividing point; you're above and you're below. You have the dimensions that you face in your mind, in your life. The Canadian night is fascinating to me. Think of our winter, our snow. In a literal way, the snow-filled Canadian night is — The clean sweep. The subtle fear. The wipe-out. The peculiar promise of a terrifying yet easy death. What a powerful metaphor it can become! But it's such a powerfully literal thing to begin with

CAMERON: In *But We Are Exiles* they try to drag the body up from below, though they don't really know why, and then when it does surface it drives everybody crazy. They're all going mad at the end of the novel.

KROETSCH: I couldn't agree more. They had it, so to speak, buried. Then up it springs on them. That's what I want to get at, that experience we have where the two meet. Mort Ross, at the University in Edmonton, once remarked that Canadians, beneath their polite surface, are all playing hockey. What the hell *is* beneath that incredible surface? Let's explore it. I don't think it's like—not like that fascinating Russian underworld that's overwhelming in its complexity. I don't think it's like the American one, which more and more becomes completely urban.

CAMERON: I wonder if there aren't some parallels with the Russian night.

KROETSCH: You know, I almost said that and then I backed down. I'm glad you said it. They have the climate, they have the space, they have the involvement in the natural world, and I think there *is* a parallel.

In *Exiles* I was trying to show how we are exiled in many ways, but in one sense from our own night.

CAMERON: So the corpse itself is for you a kind of night-world symbol?

KROETSCH: In *The Words of My Roaring* there's a man who drowns, and you get a picture of him bobbing around, floating around down there. Sort of a pleasant place—fish come nibbling at him. But Hornyak poses a threat to the living. Our relationship to the dead—Other writers have said, In our time, how do you know you're alive? You can also ask, How do you know you're dead? Hornyak is still present, functioning with the crew of the boat.

CAMERON: Interestingly, when he's shipped overboard and Peter takes his place, it's not night, but a kind of blinding vision of whiteness. So the whole business of the night world and the day world has become kind of intermingled by the end.

KROETSCH: Exactly. You remember the title comes from that poem:

> *Fair these broad meads, these hoary woods are grand—*

It's a nice idyllic picture, a Canadian boat song. But then the next line—

> *But we are exiles from our fathers' land—*

is suddenly in sharp contrast. And there you have them, day and night:

> *Fair these broad meads, these hoary woods are grand;*
> *But we are exiles from our fathers' land.*

The poet was remembering Scotland, but I'm thinking about our fathers' land as the world of the dead, of the underground, of the grave. Maybe only the dead can possess the land, make the land the "earth" again.

CAMERON: Somewhere you've written about the relationship of a family to the land, about it coming down from father to son and finally being sold by the son. Is that—

KROETSCH: That's a poem—

CAMERON: —that's right, it's *The Stone Hammer Poem*—

KROETSCH: —there's the stone hammer, on that shelf. That's the way in which—how do we know we're dead? You see that's the other side of it. We are caught in a continuity—involved, I shouldn't say "caught"— it's one of the nicest things about life, working both ways. There's a sense in which you could never exile yourself, and maybe that's what you discover after you think you've been in exile.

May 18, 1971

Robert Kroetsch:
Biography and Bibliography

*Born on the family homestead at Heisler, Alberta, in 1927,
Robert Kroetsch graduated from the University of Alberta
and went to work as a labourer in Labrador, around Hudson
Bay, and on river boats on the Mackenzie River, sandwiching
in a year of study at McGill with Hugh MacLennan. He later did
graduate study at Breadloaf College in Vermont, and at the
University of Iowa, where he obtained a Ph.D. in 1961. Since
then he has taught at the State University of New York in
Binghamton, with a year out in Alberta and another in
England. In 1969 he won the Governor General's Award for
his third novel,* The Studhorse Man. *He is married and has
two children.*

Fiction

But We Are Exiles (1965)
The Words of My Roaring (1967)
The Studhorse Man (1969)
(editor) *Creation* (1970) (with James Bacque and Pierre Gravel;
      includes excerpts from a new novel, tentatively entitled
      Funeral Games)

Non-Fiction

Alberta (1968)

Margaret Laurence:

The Black Celt Speaks of Freedom

*Margaret Laurence is a beloved friend of many years' stand-
ing—she has even dedicated a book, Jason's Quest, to my
children—and it is by no means the first time we have downed
many a cup of coffee during a long, long talk. It is not even the*

*first time this summer. In June, Timothy Findley and I finished
our interview and came, with his friend Bill Whitehead, for
dinner. Margaret and I were to do our interview that
evening; but she was deep in a novel and could not bring herself to talk about writing. Ironically, she found herself talking
of little else, and a tape of that evening's conversation would
have been extraordinarily interesting.*

*But now the summer is over, and Margaret has extracted
herself from her fictional world to wind things up for the
trip back to England. As the daylight fades across the Otonabee
River and the crickets chorus, we sit at a huge old table
before the wide window of the Panabode cabin, while she
announces she is terrified of tape recorders and microphones.
She is a tall, strong-looking woman, and though both she and
her characters are often assailed by storms of doubt and
uncertainty I have never had any real doubt of her essential
toughness of fibre, her sinewy strength of will. And her courage before the tape recorder proves a fine case in point.*

CAMERON: You once said that, looking back on your early
work, you could see the same themes you're concerned with
even now. What were they?
LAURENCE: Well, when I look back, particularly at the African
writing — at my first novel, *This Side Jordan*, and the short
stories, *The Tomorrow Tamer* — I see the whole theme of
freedom, which at that time I interpreted largely, or thought I
interpreted, in terms of political freedom — although of course
even then I realized that there was much more to it than that.
But in *This Side Jordan*, though I didn't really realize it while
I was doing it, the theme is a kind of dual freedom. Nathanial
is taking part, whether he likes it or not— and sometimes he
doesn't like it — in the move of his country toward independence, but at the same time within himself he has this enormous
battle between the old Africa and the new, and he has to come
to some kind of inner terms with his own past and with his

own fathers. The thing that really stunned me later was to look back, not only at that, but particularly at short stories like "Godman's Master", for example, where freedom is not presented in political terms, but in terms of the individual coming to terms with his own past and with himself, accepting his limitations and going on from there, however terrified he may be. When Moses, the young man, says to the dwarf, "There's more to freedom than not living in a box," Godman says, "You would not think so if you had ever lived in a box." When I went through those stories several years later, preparing to submit them for publication as a collection, it suddenly struck me that whereas I had thought at the time I was dealing with an African theme, in fact I was dealing with something which was just as much a Canadian theme and just as much a personal theme: the whole process of every human individual coming to terms with your own past, with your childhood, with your parents, and getting to the point where you can see yourself as a human individual no longer blaming the past, no longer having even to throw out all the past, but finding a way to live with your own past, which you have to do. This kind of inner freedom has been a continuing theme. I realized when I was about halfway through *The Stone Angel* that this was partly the theme there too. With Hagar, at the end of a very long and, in a sense, repressed life, part of her goal is simply survival — to survive until the moment she dies, with some kind of dignity and some kind of human value. But at the same time, the great theme at the end is the theme of freedom. She has always tried to put the hooks on people, to influence people, to manipulate them, her husband and her sons, and she has never really allowed them to go free, so she has never been free herself: this is what she comes to understand in the very last days of her life. So the theme is freedom there too, and it probably is a continuing theme in everything I have written. They say a writer's only got one theme.

CAMERON: What is it that *makes* that your theme?

LAURENCE: I don't know, Don. I think that it's very difficult to analyse. This is the theme that my life has made me, and I don't know why. It's an accumulation of every single thing that's ever happened to me, probably. It may also be a cultural thing. Having grown up in the Prairies, in a fairly stultifying community in some ways, and yet having come from, on the one hand, Scots ancestors who certainly were extremely independent if not bloody-minded, and equally bloody-minded Irish ancestors—including my grandfather about whom I've written in *A Bird in the House*, who was a terrible old man, but who had an enormous sense of his own independence—it seems to me that these two things probably have worked in kind of juxtaposition in my life: on the one hand a repressed community, on the other hand a community in which the values of the individual were extraordinarily strongly recognized, if only sometimes by implication.

CAMERON: The old man is fiercely independent, but within certain very rigid bounds.

LAURENCE: Well, he means independence for *him*, he doesn't really want independence for anybody else. He's a strong authoritarian. I really hated him as a kid, and I think with some reason: he was in some ways eminently hatable. But when I got to the end of those stories I realized that in point of fact, I was an awful lot like him in this way. I had been so rebellious against him because that very tenacity which he had, I *also* had. I feel passionate about people trying not to manipulate other people, not to force other people, and yet with my grandfather's awful example in front of me and knowing that I had the same desire for a kind of personal independence as he had, I feel that this is something in myself that I have to watch. I do not want to be an authoritarian figure as he was, but I recognize that, like Hagar, there is a good deal of the matriarch in me. I have to watch this very closely with my own kids and always have. But I don't think I ever would have known those things about myself if I hadn't written *The Stone Angel* and *A Bird in the House*.

CAMERON: Is that part of the reason for writing, to discover those things?

LAURENCE: I'm sure it is. I'm sure that all writing in that sense is a kind of self-discovery. In some profound sense there is something of you in all your characters; they are almost all of them in a way disguises for you, in one or other of your aspects, and very often you discover things about yourself through the characters that you hadn't known before. There is another very strong reason for writing, too. For quite a while, I thought that the theme of death came into my writing simply because of the number of deaths in my family when I was very young. But I think now that it's far more than that; I think that for an awful lot of writers, in fact probably most serious writers, this is some kind of quite futile way of staving off death, or, looked at in a more positive way, it could be a kind of coming to terms with the fact that you are going to die.

CAMERON: There's a lot of humour and irony in your books, but in the memory they tend to exude a sense, an almost Calvinistic sense, of the world's being a pretty tough place.

LAURENCE: I'm sure this point of view is to some extent inherited, this Presbyterian attitude toward life. I don't think that any of my fiction is all that cheery, but I certainly *hope* it has a good deal of humour in it as well, partly because I think that this is there in life, you know? I've got this terrible tendency toward what I call the Black Celt in myself, which is certainly a feeling that things could hardly be worse in the world, and that we are on the brink of a precipice. But at the same time, a sufficient number of things that happened to me have been so extraordinarily good and also so extraordinarily funny. I don't have one set of responses to life; I've got hundreds. I think every novelist probably does have.

CAMERON: Somebody observed to me recently that I was still a Puritan in that I was very hard on myself. Isn't that true of you? And also of your characters, often?

LAURENCE: I think it's extremely true of me and I think it's true of every single character that I've written about, certainly in my Canadian fiction. You just absorb it through the pores. I come from a people who feel guilty at the drop of a hat, who reproach themselves for the slightest thing, and for whom virtue arises from work: if you're not working twenty-six hours a day, you just aren't virtuous. Of course I don't believe this with my head, and I don't work twenty-six hours a day and haven't for a very long time, but at the same time I still have that uneasy feeling that I should. And also, a very odd thing: I love writing — it's both a real agony and a terrific pleasure — and because I love doing it, it took me years and years of my life to teach myself to get down to the typewriter first thing in the morning when the kids were off to school rather than making the beds, doing the dishes, cleaning the house, and blabber blabber. Not intellectually, but with some quite different part of my being, it always seemed to me that physical work was virtuous, but any kind of work like writing which you loved must be just a little — ! and that's something *very* Calvinistic.

CAMERON: If you enjoy it, it can't be work.

LAURENCE: That's right. I think this is one reason why quite purposely, over the years, I have developed a kind of idiom in this way. When I say "work", I only mean writing. It finally penetrated my thick skull, that in fact work should be something that you *love* doing, and that you put everything that you have and more into it, and that only that kind of work was really worthy of the name. So when I say "work" I only mean writing. Everything else is just odd jobs.

CAMERON: You still do work fantastically hard.

LAURENCE: I work hard when I'm working.

CAMERON: But, look, I've seen you under a fair number of circumstances, and when you're into a writing project you're sitting talking, and part of you is going right on with the work.

LAURENCE: That's absolutely true, and it's hell. I'm certainly not unique in this way. I know a great many writers, and most of them have the same hang-up. You see, it's extremely difficult to get into the work. To really make a beginning, to actually plunge in and make a start, is absolutely terrifying to me, and I can hardly bring myself to do it, and I put it off until I can't put it off any longer, till it bugs me so much I *have* to get into it. But once you get inside that fictional world, it's extraordinarily difficult to get out, and what happens, I think, is that you simultaneously lead two lives. There comes a time when you are no longer sure of which one is the more real. You have to come out of the work in order to meet your friends, relate to your family, and so on. But at the same time, the fictional world that you have momentarily left behind is just as vivid in your mind as the physical objects and even the people around you. This is very spooky; it frightens you. I find it almost impossible to shut off the voices once they start. If I stop work for, say, two or three weeks, then I'm well and truly out and then it's hell to get back in.

But as long as I am in it and writing, every day or even five days a week, I go to bed early in order to get up with the lark, refreshed: *ha ha*! I lie awake until three o'clock in the morning composing scenes in my mind which I'm too exhausted to get up and write down, or I compose things in my mind which don't happen till two-thirds of the way through the novel, and I'm crying over the death of somebody that dies in the last chapter, and this is *insanity*. You begin to feel a little odd. I get very much inside the *persona* of the main character. I'm working on a novel now, and about a week ago, I had finished work for the day, so I thought, Well, it's still only early evening, I'll write a few letters. I wrote a letter to a friend and I looked at it, and I thought, *I* didn't write that letter, *she* did. It was written in *her* idiom, *her* character, and it scared the hell out of me. I thought, Who am I? Every novelist has this terrible feeling from time to time: Who am I? because you feel almost that you may exist only in your characters and not have a character of your own. You fly to the mirror to see if you're still there. And this is really spooky.

The young writers of the generation following mine may have this less, although I wouldn't be sure. But you see I write, and most of my generation, I think, write, what I would call a Method novel. Like a Method actor, you get right inside the role. I take on, for the time I'm writing, the *persona* of the character, and I am trying to make a kind of direct connection with this person, not to manipulate them but to listen to them, to try and feel my way into their skull in such a way that I respond in the writing the way they would respond, which of course naturally is both me and not me: this is where it gets so peculiar, because it's aspects of myself and yet it's not totally me, it's them as well. They exist in their own right. I think Mordecai Richler writes this way, largely, and look at somebody like Saul Bellow: this is true of him. It's true of any number of writers of my generation. But the writers who are coming along in the next generation seem to me to want a different stance, a different point of view in which the narrator has to be present, as himself, in the novel. Some of them feel—and this is a very interesting and I think quite legitimate point of view—that for the narrator to pretend not to be there is a kind of evasion of one's responsibilities.

CAMERON: But you don't feel it as an evasion?

LAURENCE: It's the only thing that was possible for me. Things do change, thank God, from generation to generation, and this is why the novel, far from being dead, is alive and well and taking new forms. People are always announcing the death of the novel, but the novel keeps on rising like the phoenix from its own ashes. For me and for most of my generation, in Canada anyway, that kind of social realism which took in an analysis of the whole social pattern was not necessary because it had been done by people like Hugh MacLennan, like Ernest Buckler, like Sinclair Ross, and various other people—Morley Callaghan—so that when I began to write I realized quite quickly that what really grabbed me the most, what I really would like to do the most in a novel, was to, as far as possible, present the living individual on the printed page, in all his paradox and all his craziness. Of course one is attempting something that is impossible, naturally, but then every novel of whatever generation attempted something that basically is impossible, because we are not God. So, far from being a profession which is likely to make you prey to *hubris*, this is in fact a very humbling profession, because you very, very snappily realize that you are *not* God, and that whatever kind of character you put down, however strongly you feel their presence, however much you have a sense of them as human individuals, unique and irreplaceable, you can *never* put them down as interestingly or with one-millionth of the facets that the dullest person on the street has because they're *alive*. Art is never life. With my generation, the great thing was the whole exploration of personality. It was the only thing I could do. I didn't consciously set out to do it, I just did it. I didn't realize until many years later that there were influences on me other than simply personal—family and so on—but something similar seems to have happened to so many writers of my generation that I think it is more than just an individual thing.

With the young writers, perceptions have again changed, as they do from generation to generation. They don't necessarily get better or worse, but they alter. As the young writers are trying to tell us, there is not just one world; there are as many worlds as there are individuals or generations and this is what is popularly called the generation gap. It's something that has always existed, simply because once a generation, if you can put it thus crudely, the world, like a snake, sheds its skin; and for people who don't have much contact with the generation which follows them, it comes as a terrible shock to realize they are now inhabiting what is in a sense the cast-off skin of the world. In fact, of course, many people never do recognize this. It's hard to recognize, at some point, not that one is living in the past but that one was formed in a world which was very different from the present one and that the present one can be touched mainly by attempting to understand what the kids are saying. So I don't feel that I'm going to go on writing novels all my life, not because I think I've come to the end or that I'm about to give up or anything, but pretty soon I will have said what I have to say for my generation, and in my idiom and about my time and my place, which is not right now, although it's partly now in a different way, of course. But this, I think, is one reason why the work of young writers interests me so much.

CAMERON: I've noticed you review mostly new novelists.

LAURENCE: Well, I seem to have read an awful lot of novels written by young writers, particularly young Canadian writers. I do know a lot of young writers and I'm extremely interested in what they're doing, both poets and novelists. I'm telling them about my world, but they're telling me about theirs, too. It's an exchange.

CAMERON: There's a Margaret Laurence phrase that I use again and again and again; your reference to Hector "living in there behind his eyes".

LAURENCE: I suppose I feel this way myself. This is not to say that I don't believe that human beings can reach and touch one another; I know they can, because this has been my personal experience many times. But I do have the sense of a whole world going on inside each skull and I can hardly bear it that this should have to be so, because I think I want a greater sort of contact with other people than in fact may be possible. I'm sure this is one reason why I do identify so much with the main character in my books, because this character very often is, at least partly, myself, and one has this kind of perfect identification or communication in a way. I mean, I *know* what she's thinking, she *tells* me, and that sounds as though I'm off my rocker probably. It's partly that I feel that human beings ought to be able, *ought* to be able to communicate and touch each other far more than they do, and this human loneliness and isolation, which obviously occurs everywhere, seems to me to be part of man's tragedy. I'm sure one of the main themes in all my writings in this sense of man's isolation from his fellows and how almost unbearably tragic this is.

CAMERON: It's there even in the closest of relationships.

LAURENCE: Well, I'm sure it *is*. When I was very much younger I believed that total communication between two people was possible, but it isn't. At least I don't think it is. The great thing I suppose is to understand this and accept it. If it's understood

and accepted on both sides, then that is probably all right.
CAMERON: I feel surrounded by paradox when we start to talk
about this. We're talking here about things which go fairly
deep, and at the same time there are certain topics which I
would not presume to take up with you—
LAURENCE: —and I would not answer, if you did.
CAMERON: —but you *would* write about them.
LAURENCE: Of course, that's right.
CAMERON: So you communicate most fully through your art.
LAURENCE: One of the paradoxes of every writer is that however restrained and even reticent a person one may be—and
many writers are—what you are not willing to say to your
friends about your responses to life, you will declare in front
of the whole world in black and white, which is absurd. But
of course it's partly the whole question of the characters in the
novel not entirely being oneself; they are aspects of oneself,
but there are so *many* aspects. You don't ever get them all
across in one character, and different things happen to the
character to the events of your own personal life. But what
you are doing in many cases obviously is to put down, as far
as you can see with your own eyes, some of your basic responses to life—which has nothing to do with the *external*
events of the novel. When people ask me if what I've written is
autobiographical, it isn't, except in the case of the stories in
A Bird in the House, which are directly drawn from my own
childhood although even there fictionalized—but nothing I
have written is directly autobiographical at all. The thing that
is autobiographical is not the events, not the characters, but
some of the underlying responses toward life, where you're
really saying what you really feel about various human situations.
CAMERON: This project is fascinating in just that way, because you're meeting people you know reasonably well
before you've ever laid an eye on them.
LAURENCE: I've felt this many times, meeting writers for the
first time when I've been familiar with their work; and if

they've been familiar with mine, we meet almost as old friends.

CAMERON: It really does work as communication.

LAURENCE: Yes. The difference — if there is that much difference — between a writer and an inmate at a mental hospital is only that in the case of the writer you are going at some point to open the door of your private world and ask other people to come in. The private world is ultimately meant to communicate, to turn outward, not to keep on turning inward. For all I know, this is why many writers maintain a vestige of their sanity, so-called.

CAMERON: D. H. Lawrence once said that one sheds one's sicknesses in one's books. It sounds like a psycho-therapeutic exercise.

LAURENCE: It is, in part, for every writer. The thing one has to be quite clear about is that if it is *only* a therapeutic exercise, for God's sake put it in the bottom drawer. Therapy is a perfectly legitimate reason to write, but it doesn't make literature.

CAMERON: What *does?*

LAURENCE: As soon as I said that, I knew I shouldn't have.

CAMERON: Well, there's a simpler way of getting at it. When you reject something, on what grounds do you reject it? What makes you decide to stage one of the celebrated Margaret Laurence manuscript burnings in the back yard at Penn?

LAURENCE: Well. I always remember what Mordecai Richler said, that the writer really only had one responsibility, and that was not to bore the reader. I think that it has to interest me intensely before it can interest anybody else intensely. It has to have some kind of inner life of its own which I find very hard to describe, and I find very hard to formulate standards which will communicate what I mean. It has to have a certain form, although that's less important than its inner life. Life is extraordinarily, and in a way wonderfully, formless, and yet the whole world sort of examined minutely has got incredible form. I don't personally care for novels which are enormously verbose and rambling, with a great deal of flesh but, as it were, no skeleton.

CAMERON: How often do you have that experience of having written something, and looking at it and saying, No? And is that more common now or less than at the beginning?

LAURENCE: It's always been pretty common, Don. With almost everything I've written I have done a great deal of rewriting, and in many cases I've thrown away sizable portions and had to start over again. When I wrote *The Fire Dwellers*, for example, I must have made at least three, if not four, separate starts on it. The first time was many years ago in Vancouver, even before I began writing *A Jest of God*, and it just didn't work. I started again when I went to England in '63, and I wrote about two or three chapters, but it was really awful. It just didn't come together at all. Then, after I had finished writing *A Jest of God*, I started again. I knew it was there, only it was just that I hadn't found it yet. I must have written about a hundred pages or more and I could see that it just was not coming across, so I burned those hundred pages and then I really wanted to go and hang myself. However, I put it away then for a while, and did something else, and when I got it out finally after about the fourth try, maybe I'd learned enough, maybe even thought about it enough, subconsciously. I hadn't been ready to write it before, obviously.

I don't mind that, I don't mind that a bit. I mind at the *time*, obviously; I feel like hell; but what I mind far more than having to chuck out two or three chapters or start again on something I'm convinced *is* there, what I do mind is when I have started a book which actually was *not* really there, that I couldn't keep on with because it just turned out to be the wrong thing and I didn't feel strongly enough about it, or something about it meant I couldn't write it. This has happened three times, I guess, and this is a really depressing experience, the books that don't get written. One shouldn't be depressed because they would have turned out rotten books, but at the time it's terrible because you think you'll never write again.

It's the international neurosis of writers. As a novelist friend of mine once said, In between novels you feel with the passionate conviction of despair that you will never write another word.

CAMERON: But you do, eventually. When you say you have a sense of a novel being there, how far in advance does that go? Did you have any sense, way back when, of how many novels were there?

LAURENCE: No, I don't think I knew that, but right from the time I began writing *This Side Jordan*, I've always known what two books were next. They weren't completely formed, mind you, and sometimes it takes years for them to be ready to be written. I think sometimes that the whole process of invention, or of getting to know a character, almost takes place at a subconscious level. If you've got a particular character in mind, once you really start thinking about it or even when you're not consciously thinking of it, various things that happen to you, or that you read, or that you perceive, or overhear in people's conversations, and so on, are all mentally channelled into that area. Characters can be years in my head, and usually are, before I really start writing about them.

CAMERON: Is that a finite pot of novels? Either out of desperation or conviction, you've suggested that you can see an end to the process of novel-writing.

LAURENCE: Well, I don't really see any novels beyond the one that I'm writing now. There's a kids' book that I'd like to write after I finish this novel, if it happens that way, but I don't see any more novels. Still, the whole process can take you by surprise, so that when I say I don't think there will be any more novels after this one — if I'm lucky enough to be able to finish it — I could be wrong. I just don't know. I've been very wrong before in the various statements I've made about my writing. For years every time I finished a book I would say, Well, this is absolutely the last time that I will ever write anything at all which comes out of that Prairie town. Before I started this novel that I'm working on, I swore up and down that there was

no way that Manawaka was going to come into it at all. Well,
I've got about a third of the way through the first draft, and
we've just now got out of the town. I don't even care any more.
I think, Well okay, I'm lumbered with it.

CAMERON: You must feel you're at the mercy of forces
which you don't really know or understand.

LAURENCE: That's true. Of course because writers do say
this and it is true, people sometimes get the impression that
writers believe there is a sort of mystique about writing, something very strange, and I hate to sound that way. Yet in a profound sense it's true: in a way you *are* at the mercy of forces
that you don't understand. People like the ancient Greeks or
even the Africans of a slightly earlier time than now didn't
have the slightest problem explaining this kind of thing, with
a carver, with an actor, with a dramatist, because it was simply
that they were possessed by the god: it was a very simple concept which gave them no trouble at all. In our present culture,
which is so scientifically oriented, you talk in those terms and
they send you to the nut-house. But it's only a sort of verbal
expression. When somebody said, in African tribal society or
in Ancient Greece, that they were possessed by the god, this
was simply another way of saying, I suppose, that there
were forces in your subconscious, — and in the whole sort of
cultural pool of which your mind is a part and by which it has
been formed — that are shaping you, out of which you're
drawing this kind of material. In a sense it is mysterious because it's something you can't totally analyse and don't totally
understand, and indeed do not *need* to understand. I don't
have to understand what makes me write a novel or where
my characters come from. All I have to be able to do, God
willing, is do it.

So it doesn't really matter in what terms you explain it, but
you do have this sense of doing something which is to some
extent beyond your conscious control. I suppose my writing so
much out of that Prairie town — which is partly my own town
and partly a town of the mind, a fictional town — my reasons

for having to keep on doing it are unimportant, but they're valid as long as this comes across as a real inner necessity for me. I have a very strange feeling about that fictional town, Manawaka, because when a particular name occurs to me, for example, I have to stop and think, Now was that family in the town of Neepawa, Manitoba, or was that family in the fictional town of Manawaka? I sometimes get them confused, and I'm not quite sure which is which. I also find with the fictional town that there are various characters who have occurred in almost everything that I've written with a Canadian setting. Some of the families in that town have had very minor parts in various novels, and some of them I find recurring. They pop up again, you know, and I think, Oh yeah, it's old so-and-so again; and I have this strange sense of knowing a great many families in a fictional town for three generations. For example, in the novel that I'm writing now, when a certain lawyer comes into it, I'll think, Of course that would have to be Simon Pearl, that would be old Henry's son. Well, Henry was a farmer who was a friend of Hagar's in *The Stone Angel*, but who also died of pneumonia in one of the stories in *A Bird in the House*. This kind of relationship. I don't force it there, it just *is* there. It's kind of a strange feeling, because you honestly do have this sense of intimate genealogical knowledge of this particular place — which is a *fictional* place. And here are all these people you know, walking around in your head, and their grand-children! How long can this go on? I'm being taken over!

CAMERON: You're possessed by the god. Of course your fictional world is not devoid of what has been known as religion.

LAURENCE: I think that I see not only my characters but myself and everybody else in a world which is not devoid of religion. I don't have any feeling, personally, of loyalty to the traditional Christian religions, and I say religions advisedly. I think of myself as a kind of religious atheist, if you like, or religious agnostic, who knows? but I do not really believe that God is totally dead in our universe, you see. I don't know even what I mean by God, but I don't think, personally, that we do live in a universe which is as empty as we might think. A lot of my characters, like myself, inhabit a world in which they no longer believe in the teachings of the traditional church, but where these things have enormous emotional impact on them still, as they do on me. There's a great deal, for example, in the Bible which really hits me very hard; it seems to express certain symbolic truths about the human dilemma and about mankind. The expression of various facets of human life and of human life searching for a consciousness greater than its own — that is, in God — some of this moves me in the way that great poetry moves you. I'm particularly attached to the King James version of the Bible, because it *is* the poetry of it that really hits me. A great many of the characters feel as I do about it: there's an enormous emotional inheritance. I am a Christian in the sense of my heritage. I'm capable as most novelists are, perhaps as most people are, of holding two mutually exclusive points of view at the same time, so that I can absolutely detest, intellectually, the thought behind a hymn like "Onward Christian Soldiers", while I still think this is one of the most stirring and wonderful hymns ever written. Part of the terrific impact of things like the hymns derives from the fact that you learned these things in a much earlier era of your life, an era of rock-solid faith. Now you *lost* this: and part of the impact is not that you believe it, but you mourn your disbelief. This is Eden lost.

CAMERON: The action of time fascinates you, doesn't it? And it's not just growth, but history, too. Look at the Manawaka novels as a group: there's an obvious historical flow through those novels.

LAURENCE: Oh, of course there is. When you take it right up to Stacey's children in *The Fire Dwellers*, it covers four generations: my grandparents' generation, my parents' generation, my own generation, and my children's generation, and in fact this is the historical span of my writing. Interestingly enough,

I think you would find in the writing of Chinua Achebe the exact same historical span.

CAMERON: That *is* interesting, isn't it? And in Roch Carrier, too.

LAURENCE: That's right, you do. He's a splendid writer, isn't he? I'm sure that many novelists find this an almost essential process, when they really start writing deeply out of their own background, when they really think that there's no evasion, you've got to just do it. When I started writing *The Stone Angel*, that's when it hit me like the spirit of God between the eyes. I didn't really intend to start writing a novel set in that generation, but I suddenly realized that this was the place where I had to start, in a sense, with my grandparents' generation.

CAMERON: That's the oldest experience of which you can get a first-hand report.

LAURENCE: That's precisely why. Beyond that you have repeated tales which become myths of your great-grandparents, but you don't personally remember them. You haven't personally heard their idiom, or their stories. Beyond your great-grandparents, as I have frequently said before, the ancestors become everybody's ancestors. They're kind of a diffuse, anonymous lot who you sometimes see in old family albums and wonder who they were, but you have no means of knowing. It all becomes myth at that point. But with your grandparents, though it's a myth too, it's so much closer and more vivid, particularly in cases where you have known your own grandparents, or known their generation. I remember when I wrote *The Stone Angel* what a terrific surprise it was to me to realize that I was actually writing a lot of Hagar's speech in the idiom of my grandparents' generation—which was, I may say, an idiom which I didn't even know I remembered until it came back to me with her, and I *knew* it was right. It was like tapping a part of your head that you didn't know was there, and it was all there.

CAMERON: That very simple definition you gave a while ago that what you were trying to do with the novel, basically, was to get the characters down right; that implies a tremendously wide and various ambition. Do you think of yourself as an ambitious writer?

LAURENCE: I don't think there's any point in being anything else. Sure I'm ambitious—not in the sense that I want to write a best-seller, although I'd be delighted if I did—but ambitious in what I am attempting to do, certainly. *Extremely* ambitious, because—Heavens, let's not deceive ourselves—to try and get down some of the paradoxes of any human individual with everything that has gone to influence their life—their parents, the whole bit about history, religion, the myth of the ancestors, the social environment, their relationships with other people and so on— even to *attempt* it means attempting the impossible. What comes to mind always in this regard, and I'm sure that it's true, is Graham Greene's sentence. In one of his essays, he said: "For the serious writer, as for the priest, there is no such thing as success."

September 14, 1971

Margaret Laurence:
Biography and Bibliography

Margaret Wemyss was born in Neepawa, Manitoba, in 1926, and became Margaret Laurence when she married Jack Laurence, a civil engineer, after graduating from the University of Manitoba. His work took them to England, British Somaliland, Ghana, and Vancouver. In 1963 she moved back to England with her two children, coming to rest in a rambling old house in Penn, Buckinghamshire, near High Wycombe. In 1969 the Laurences were divorced, and Mrs. Laurence now lives in Penn with the children during the winter, spending her summers in a riverside cottage near Peterborough, Ontario.

Fiction

This Side Jordan (1960)
The Tomorrow Tamer and Other Stories (1963)
The Stone Angel (1964)
A Jest of God (1966) (paperback title: *Rachel, Rachel*)
The Fire-Dwellers (1969)
A Bird in the House (1970)
Jason's Quest (for children) (1970)

Non-Fiction

A Tree for Poverty: Somali Poetry and Prose (1954; repr. 1970)
The Prophet's Camel Bell (1963) (U.S. title: *New Wind in a Dry Land*)
Long Drums and Cannons: Nigerian Dramatists and Novelists 1952-1966 (1968)

Criticism

Clara Thomas, Margaret Laurence (1969)
W. E. Swayze, Margaret Laurence (*in preparation*)

Jack Ludwig:

Sleeping Is a Criminal Activity

Fifteen miles into Long Island from Manhattan, Roslyn Estates is an older development, winding, leafy, and prosperous. Jack Ludwig rises from his lawn chair near the patio with some difficulty. A childhood disease kept him in traction for four years, and his hip is still affected. But his vitality is so obvious, his eagerness to involve himself in talk is so clear, his energy and shrewdness are so evident in the expressions that chase over his face, that he seems dramatically better endowed than most people.

We decide to record the interview outside, at the patio table, but the air is racketing with the sound of four or five neighbouring power mowers. It's like this every Saturday, Ludwig explains, but it's over by two o'clock. It will be quiet after that until four thirty, when the orioles will start singing in the garden trees. Tell me all about your book.

By two, the final lawnmower has indeed spluttered down into silence, and we begin talking—though the tape is punctuated by the repeated wail of sirens near by, a reminder that even in this green garden we are only a few miles from the rotting, violent purlieus of Fun City, U.S.A. Squinting in the sun, the wind ruffling his greying hair, Ludwig nods briskly in agreement, frowns when he disagrees, laughs heartily and often. He is frankly enjoying himself, enjoying the exchange of ideas, briskly ruminating. So I enjoy myself too. Good company, and good talk: what better way could there be to spend a sunny May afternoon?

CAMERON: You've worked a lot with theatre and TV. Is that satisfying, or does something in you still cry out to put words down on paper?

LUDWIG: Oh, always. Oh sure. You go through a few days without writing something, you go out of your mind, so you carry little books with you. They're just full of scribbles and scratches. Some of them have to do with novels, some have to do with short stories, and some have to do with poems. Some have to do with a political situation, some have to do with just an observation, some kind of miraculous thing that's happened in front of your eyes, and that may not make it into fiction but it doesn't make it any less important or even less of an event in your life. A lot of the stuff that you jot down and you see and experience never gets into literature. That isn't its test. I mean the test is *it*, not you or literature. It has the first call.

CAMERON: You said earlier on that when you went to California you knew you wanted to write.

LUDWIG: Yeah, I'd been writing from the time that I was in grade school, writing and setting up magazines, newspapers, and things. This was just a level that was almost casual. There were no questions that had to be asked about it; it was just going to go on.

CAMERON: But it was still the best part of twenty years before *Confusions*. What did you write during that time? *Thoreau in California* for one thing.

LUDWIG: That, incidentally, has had a tremendous vogue in the last two or three years. It's just been reprinted, just in the last eighteen months, in about four or five different anthologies, mostly in the United States, and it's also been included in the *Proceedings* of the Thoreau Society! Well, a lot of the stuff that I wrote actually appeared in *Above Ground*. A lot of the things that are in *Above Ground* I worked on for a long time prior to the time that I began working on *Confusions*. That material wasn't connected in any way, except as a kind of linked sequence of stories with the same central character, with the analogue of Joyce's *Dubliners* standing behind it. I put that aside and finished *Confusions*, then I picked it up right after. *Confusions* actually had been finished about four years before it came out, but it went through a series of very interesting stunts with publishers during that time. It actually shifted publishers three times before it came out.

CAMERON: How did that happen?

LUDWIG: One part is too long and too mysterious to explain. The second change, which brought it to the place that actually published it, was brought on by the publisher's saying the book was obscene and my refusing to accept that. His judgement that it was obscene came at roughly the same time that *Tropic of Cancer* had just passed its court test, and I thought that his timing was quite poor. I got the dean of a law school to read it and in his opinion it was definitely not obscene; and the idea that a publisher would call something obscene rather than wait for a cop or some kind of flag-waving lunatic with a smut-fix is just beyond me.

CAMERON: Can you explain Winnipeg to me? That city has produced an incredible number of writers, and a ballet company, and a theatre company and so on.

LUDWIG: I don't know what the answer can be about the relationship between a place and the activity that goes on there. From my own point of view, there was something that had to be rescued out of Winnipeg. The concrete nature of the experience that you had there, and the fact that everything was so absolutely three-dimensional, and the fact that it seemed to be passing, made it almost an imperative for writers to do something with that world before it just went away; and in doing something with that particular fleeting world they may have discovered something about the world that wasn't so fleeting. I just recently wrote a thing for the hundredth anniversary of Manitoba, part of an issue of *Mosaic*, saying that you *must* go home again. It has to do with how you change your attitude towards things, so that horse-play and satiric and ironic poses are fine, and writing things off, but ultimately those things are *there* in your past. Even after you've written them off you keep coming back to them and back to them and back to them. There's something else there, and the thing that's there is the challenge to your imagination to face something that isn't the obvious kind of satiric thing, that isn't the obvious kind of wipe-out. The metaphor I was using there was the Golden Boy on the legislative buildings, which was always the biggest bloody joke to me, except that when you fix it in time and in space and you have things going on around it and under it, it becomes something entirely different. It really does become transformed by the imagination. Probably the great thing about a city like Winnipeg was all its contradictions and all the sounds that you heard there, all the different tones. I grew up on a street where there were Ukrainians and Poles on either side of me; there was a Scot with an incredible brogue about two houses down; a guy with the most unbelievable Raj accent, who had spent a lot of time in India, across the street; a labourer from Belgium, some Germans, some Swiss people, a Jewish tailor whose son was a violinist right out of Isaac Babel's Odessa, this kind of thing. One household, just about the day we moved there, the cops swooped down on. The mother was a madam, a couple of daughters were whoring. They were replaced, incidentally, by a member of the city school board, so respectability hit us in a big hurry. Everything was there, everything was in the schools that I attended, and you just used the language, you used the sounds that you heard, because the sounds were really incredibly varied.

CAMERON: *Requiem for Bibul* comes out of that milieu.

LUDWIG: That was the first time I really tried to lay out what that experience was. I wrote that in Winnipeg too, in a very funny way. I was back there writing *Confusions*, and I set it aside for two afternoons and wrote *Bibul* in two afternoons. Before those two afternoons I'd gone home by way of an old lane, and this whole thing had just come flooding back from the image of the lane. There's a lot if it left to do. I've got all sorts of things with just Winnipeg as the background still going.

CAMERON: Offbeat question, maybe a frivolous question, but why does the smell of toasted sesame have an erotic connotation for you?

LUDWIG: Erotic?

CAMERON: Yeah.

LUDWIG: (through bursts of startled and delighted laughter): Oh, that's *marvellous!* Ha ha — oh all I can tell you is that there is an answer — ha ha — and it is not a frivolous question.

CAMERON: There's not an answer for publication?

LUDWIG: (still laughing): That's right. But you're in New York, I'll tell you what to do. Go to the Near East Bakery, around three o'clock in the morning when they're baking. It's on Atlantic Avenue in Brooklyn Heights, just between Clinton and Court. That's when you'll smell sesame. How to make it erotic I leave to you.

CAMERON: What about the experience of being in the States? In *Canadian Literature* a few years ago, you said if you were going to belong to a tradition, it was not going to be Mazo de la Roche or Stephen Leacock, it was going to be the wider tradition.

LUDWIG: That doesn't mean it's the States, I mean it —

CAMERON: — all right, but it's a metropolitan centre.

LUDWIG: I can have more connection with Julio Cortazar at this stage of the game than I can have with Mazo de la Roche. Or Kafka, or Kierkegaard, or Nietzsche, on a literary, cultural, and artistic level. But because that is true doesn't mean that passing, as I did last summer, Mazo de la Roche's house I didn't have a real thing going for that particular physical place. I can't stand reading her, but as something that is happening in Canada, and something that I have a reaction to, it's totally different. It's localized in a way. I have it in other places too, but it's very very intense in Canadian places.

CAMERON: Of course, if you are fifteen miles from Manhattan it's surely easy to be *au fait* with what's going on.

LUDWIG: Yeah, but since I came back from Canada, I've cut myself off from that world. People who are close friends of mine, writers, film-makers, and people like that, in some cases I haven't even spoken to them since I came back. These are people I used to see all the time. The whole literary thing has changed a lot. The political feeling in the country has just deteriorated so much in the last four or five years that whatever literary life there was then seems grossly irrelevant now, quite beside the point.

CAMERON: Margaret Laurence says she sometimes feels desperate about being a novelist in such a time. We're faced with cataclysmic problems and here I sit telling stories.

LUDWIG: Well, nothing compels you to just sit and tell

stories; and of course Margaret *doesn't* just sit and tell stories. When I was in London, Margaret was as concerned as the rest of us were in what then developed as the Biafran situation. She had special knowledge and special talents that she used. The new situation is that sixty years ago a writer could think, as Yeats thought, that you really had to keep yourself out of politics, you really had to keep yourself out of the hysteria of the moment in order to do your work, but I don't think people have that feeling any more. In the present time people think they have to do something, they really *have* to do something, and whatever talents you have as a writer have to be translated into action in some particular way. This organization that I worked with in Toronto is called Praxis, and the word is the key thing, that notion of praxis. If your novels or your poems or your short stories can be as involved in practice as what you do about particular crises, okay. But if they can't, you can't be coerced by the moment into giving up what it is that you are doing in your fiction and your writing generally. All the same, this is no time for a novelist, a writer, not to look into the paper, look at television, or go out on the streets and see what is happening.

CAMERON: You have to trust your own imagination to be looking at things which are relevant even at times when it would appear that they aren't?

LUDWIG: Right. Of course, you start with something relevant and then it may not be that relevant because it takes a long time to do serious, involved fiction writing. Then comes the business of having the courage to stay with the thing that you were doing. The nature of time, now, is that everything is converted into a historical novel by tomorrow. You might as well relax and accept it that way.

CAMERON: So I'd guess you're working on another novel.

LUDWIG: I'm working on *two* other novels. The novel that I'm just touching up has sort of grown out of *A Woman of Her Age*, that story that's set in Montreal, and it's about five characters from whose point of view more or less the same action is seen as in the original short story. I'm writing another novel that's completely different from that, about an electronic genius who wants everything brought to a baroque unified vision, so that every single moment is an engagement for all the senses, for all the media, the flesh, the soul, the mind. His tentative conclusion about himself is that he's impossible to live with.

CAMERON: The manic laughter of that is very like your early work. Are you going back to that vein?

LUDWIG: Oh, I have no desire to get back to that. When I look at it now, particularly if I look at *Thoreau in California*, I knock myself out laughing, but at the same time, there's nothing about that I really want to do again. It isn't that I spurn it in any way; I'm delighted with it. With that amount of time between the moment you write something and the moment you see it again, it is as though it's done by somebody else and it's fascinating to read it in that particular way. Certain things that you think of as brand new, or really formulations of the moment, are right there. You've been thinking about this particular kind of thing for a long, long time. I can see where the kind of feeling I have about things now is directly connected with the line from the first story I published, *A Woman of Her Age*, through *Confusions* to *Above Ground*, and a story Mordecai's just brought out in the Penguin series, which hadn't been published in this country before — it had been published in London — called *Einstein and This Admirer*, which is about the last day that I spent with Dylan Thomas. There's a tremendous continuity that you can discover, both about the way you feel about language and the way you feel about things that are funny and not funny. Nothing ultimately is there because it is funny by itself. The funny thing always goes somewhere, it's always trying to see something. So that that sense of the absurd, or that sense of the possibilities of language, is still there at this stage, but the kind of demand that is made on the level of reality out of which this concern comes is much higher now than it was when *Confusions* was written.

In *Confusions*, it could be a kind of stylistic lark, but now it just can't be. One of the things that this electronic genius does is periodically take to his death bed, and he has a whole thing about how you're supposed to die and what you're supposed to say. He knows everybody's last words and what the circumstances were for everybody's death, how the ideal death should be created in this way. So he's crazy, he's nuts, he's absurd—but at the same time he's coming to the great existential question. I mean, the guy really is impossible to live with—?

CAMERON: —then surely he's got to know how to die.

LUDWIG: Yes. That's a pretty serious discovery.

CAMERON: Who are the writers you care about? What books would you value above all?

LUDWIG: Well, there are books that you absolutely live with, and they probably order the way you look at things in the twenty-four hours of a day—*Don Quixote*, that kind of book. Quite apart from all the horse-play and all the satire and all the jokes, you just come back to it over and over and over again, and it's as though you re-read it every day too—you don't, but you remember things that he's got in there, the doubleness, and the acceptance of the doubleness, the range of compassion, and the fantastic way in which reality is transmogrified. To me the writer is the guy who pays attention to how you get through the twenty-four-hour day, on a second-to-second, minute-by-minute basis. There's no generalization for existence. Everything is a sum of particulars; every second is ticked off with something happening to mark the time, and Cervantes is just a great guy on that score. That book just comes back and back and back and back and there's just a deepening sense of what he is about and what he is able to see. Even more so than Shakespeare. That's a heretical thing to say.

CAMERON: I sensed a drift towards Shakespeare, though.

LUDWIG: Well, of course. The point about Shakespeare is that you do exactly the same thing with him, during the course of the day, even when you're not teaching. You explain something by using an example from Shakespeare. There are moments in the plays that have become part of your own experience, and you carry them the way you carry your corpuscles. I think the moment of Osric bringing Hamlet the challenge and Hamlet then turning and talking to Horatio about what it's all about: you've had the grave-diggers scene, you've gone through that whole thing, it's just one of those human bust-outs. From my point of view it had nothing to do with art; it just had to do with a level of recognition that's so astounding that you just sort of shiver for the rest of your life, after you've come across it the first time. When it comes down to people like Kafka, Kierkegaard, Nietzsche, it isn't ever, in my own experience, a whole work or all the works by somebody. It's the moments in a particular work. There'll be some little thing in Dostoevsky's diary, or some little thing in a Kafka short story, or just a descriptive thing. I was struck a short while ago by picking up Borges again and reading something about how the shadows in a railway car fall differently on a guy's face as he keeps travelling because the sun is in a different position to the car from when the shadows start to fall, and something like that just overwhelms me; it's so fantastically beautiful because it's so fantastically simple, easy, and the guy who has the imagination to stop on those moments is just a fantastic character. There are things in Borges that bore the hell out of me, and I wouldn't want to spend a minute going back over them — but then comes something so fantastically illuminating that you don't care that it's taken you four days to get there.

CAMERON: You don't think in terms of the over-all conception.

LUDWIG: I do, but that's not from a writer's point of view. In teaching things or talking to people about things I do that, but in something like Proust, where you've got twenty-two hundred pages of something that is very involved and fantastic — really a magnificent book; for me it doesn't have a moment of lapse in it — even there, from the writer's point of view there

126   *Conversations with Canadian Novelists*

still are just these tiny little things that stand out that have to
do with the way a particular person is dressed, or moving
through space, or related to an explanation of impressionistic
painting or something just by a specific detail, or by the way
sounds come in, and that's the literature of men. It's not the
literature of literature. Or take somebody like Yeats, who's
what the Supreme Court would call a hard case. He is not the
kind of guy that you would like to spend any time with; he is
not a very ingratiating character, and yet the poetry is just so
phenomenal. The only two poets I can think of where there's
no lapse or lag are Donne and Yeats. You're in contact with an
extraordinary imagination. The guy who says we must labour
to be beautiful is a guy that you want to think about for a long,
long time.

CAMERON: What did you read as a kid?

LUDWIG: I read Dickens as a child, and the usual stuff.
During the Depression an uncle of mine who had lost his job
in a bank moved into the house, and he had one of Eliot's five-
foot shelves, and so what I read was what was on that shelf.
Balzac and Maupassant and never Flaubert, because Flaubert
wasn't on that shelf, and a certain amount of Dickens and
some George Eliot, things like *Lorna Doone*. I don't think they
had very much lasting effect. They were just gobbled up and
all sorts of other things were being gobbled up with them.
Newspapers were being gobbled up, especially sports. I
spent a lot of time in hospitals, not walking, so that I find even at
this stage of the game I'm absolutely appalled by the fact that
I'll know everything about everybody in all sports, including
horses. You find that you know how many assists Frank
Mahovlich had with the Red Wings or what the scrap was with
Punch Imlach, those absolutely irrelevant, going-nowhere
details.

CAMERON: Just for the times you were in the hospital?

LUDWIG: It lasted, once it got started. It just had, and still
has, a life of its own. I feel I have sort of an autonomous sports-
watching self, that seems to be quite independent of me,

thank you, and it's always in business, always in business. I probably read the sports page first. One of the reasons for it now is that it's probably the only place in the newspaper where you can get information you can believe. If they tell you the score was 3-2 yesterday, you really can believe it. I can't think of any other source that I would believe at this stage. I don't even believe the newspaper telling you what ships are coming in.

CAMERON: Have any of these interests fallen away?

LUDWIG: I can't think of any specific interest that I ever had at any time that has ever fallen away. Time just doesn't have an existence for me; as a result everything is just rushing along at the same speed.

CAMERON: You have a kind of omnivorous quality, that you've been going around sort of gobbling up everything in sight.

LUDWIG: Yeah — grab it! I remember a marvellous discovery. Years ago — I guess I was still an undergraduate in Manitoba, may have still been in high school — I found out about the stuff that Kafka read, and the stuff that Kafka read was such shit you couldn't believe it. I mean there was just no scale to it whatsoever. He was reading the worst kind of stuff that Franz Werfel was writing at the time, or that Wassermann was writing at the time. On my list, Kafka being way at the top somewhere, guys like Werfel and Wassermann were way down at the bottom, and the idea that my Kafka would spend his time with those jerks was unbelievable. But I started to see that he didn't have any concern for ranking or rating, that in every instance there was a specific thing that he admired, even in an unrealized story or unrealized moment. He had the wisdom to keep his eyes open and know that you don't get yourself faked out by what's fashionable, what's supposed to be in, because that's the way you really lose everything. You don't go along with what seems to be relevant at a particular moment, but at the same time you pay attention to what people consider to be relevant, because the fact that they consider it to be relevant is an important event in itself. I want to know everything and grab everything, experience everything, be everywhere, preferably at the same time.

CAMERON: Doesn't this tear you apart?

LUDWIG: Oh, sure. It just means that your twenty-four-hour day has to be a twenty-four-hour day and any time that you take away from it for sleeping or something is just criminal activity. Two or three hours of sleep is more than anybody should be losing from what's going on. Listen! there's the oriole.

CAMERON: Right on time.

LUDWIG: It's only four-twenty. He's ten minutes early.

May 22, 1971

Jack Ludwig:
Biography and Bibliography

Jack Ludwig was born in Winnipeg in 1922, and was subjected to his early education in the public schools and, during extended periods of illness, by private tutoring. He graduated from the University of Manitoba and later earned the Ph.D. at the University of California in Los Angeles. He has taught at Williams College, and at the University of Minnesota; he is now professor of English at the State University of New York campus at Stony Brook, Long Island. During 1967-8 he was writer-in-residence at the University of Toronto. His many short stories have won several prizes and have been widely reprinted. He lives with his wife and two children in Roslyn Estates, Long Island.

Fiction

Confusions (1963)
Above Ground (1968)

Non-Fiction

Recent American Novelists
(editor, with Andy Wainwright) *Soundings* (1970)

Hugh MacLennan :

The Tennis Racket Is an Antelope Bone

*The Arts Building at McGill exudes that slightly dignified
shabbiness characteristic of old Canadian halls of learning.
The door off the staircase landing would seem to lead to a
closet, but behind it is a room less like an office than a rather*

gracious study in a private home.

Hugh MacLennan is comfortable in slacks and a V-neck sweater. Slighter and wirier than his pictures suggest, he moves with the grace of a former athlete. A hereditary classicist, with a Rhodes Scholarship and a Princeton Ph.D. in Roman history behind him, this urbane Montrealer has never ceased to be a Cape Breton Scot, and his talk preserves the warm lilt of his Gaelic ancestors. He has a knack of making the interviewer feel important: give him half a chance and he would turn the interview around, putting shrewd questions and listening respectfully to the answers. "You were at Berkeley, then? When? Ah, before it blew up. What did you think of it?"

We disagreed on politics; without much effort we could have disagreed violently; yet somehow it would have remained within the family. The most Canadian of our novelists, MacLennan remains without contradiction very much a Scot, and so do I. Not surprisingly, our conversation is dominated by a pawky, droll humour, perfectly expressed in the MacLennan smile, which the tape recorder cannot capture: open-mouthed in the front, as if with indrawn breath, and tilting up to the peaked corners of the mouth, it seems to terminate at the pointed tips of the ears. Accompanied by an impish glint in the hooded eyes, it converts MacLennan into a boyish version of Auld Cloutie.

CAMERON: Critics always make this point about the centrality of the national question in your novels, but it's always seemed to me that they were not about that at all, that they were about fathers and sons, and justice, and themes of that kind.

MACLENNAN: I think that's perfectly correct. To quote one of my own characters, all politics begins in the nursery. This business of nationalism has always bothered me more than it's bothered most modern writers. It was a convenient peg for a certain type of superficial critic: I say superficial justifiably, because all fiction has got a national base in the French sense of the word, *la nation*. When I started writing this was an unrecognizable country to the world and to itself; somebody had to do something like this. Aristotle said drama depends upon recognition, and if there are no recognitions there is no drama. In Canada it is not necessary to anything like the same extent now. I'm writing a novel based in Montreal now, and the name Montreal isn't mentioned till about page seven.

CAMERON: But the other themes are hardly obsolete.

MACLENNAN: The situations, the themes that I have happened to latch onto — don't ask me how they occurred, because this is mysterious to me too. Regardless of what Toronto critics would say, I think mature readers, and men of experience — I'm not looking at literary critics here — would generally think that the best books I had done were the last two. But the difficulty with my last novel, *Return of the Sphinx*, was that people when they read it didn't know what it was all about. It was a dramatic novel, the most dramatic I ever wrote. I didn't know when I wrote it — I started in 1963 — that within a few year's time we would find overwhelming evidence of case after case like this. I'd never heard of Vallières, but Vallières was a spoiled priest, just like my character Latendresse; he was two years in a seminary to become a Franciscan, born poor and not too sure where he was. I didn't know that some of the highest public men here had sons who were separatists. Some of them were judges and lawyers, a few were politicians. The girl Lise Balcer who's in jail now is the niece of Léon Balcer, and her father was a war hero. This is a curious thing. I happen to believe in the God that's implicit in evolution, and when you find such a fantastic break in the human psyche as happened in the 1960s, well — If a nation or a group of people threatens all species, something *happens*. Now you have an American army that won't fight, and this is not accidental. This is part of the chain of life, as I see it. It's away above politics.

CAMERON: Is this a psychological matter, or a historical one? Or are they the same thing?

MACLENNAN: I think our ancestors would call it divine, when they said that God is not mocked. I don't want to be too theological here, but scientists tell me that in human and ordinary terms it's not inaccurate. We may assume that evolution is now a provable fact. It has been amply proved and fairly closely dated what our animal origin is. The thinking part of the human brain, which became so large, grew on top of the old animal brain and in this situation you have light and dark, you have the law of Eros and Thanatos. There you have God and Satan, right in there. There's everlasting confusion and conflict between them. So the poets were right all the time, and the environmentalists are up the creek. If, therefore, one believes in evolution — and we're only using anthropomorphic terms — why should not one assume that what our ancestors called God also evolved? He thought as a mathematician, anthropomorphically speaking, when he was young. He was noisy and he blew things up, and he was interested in gases and all these ferocious things, just like the people in the AEC. But later on there developed living organisms and in these you find a complete mockery of all rational plans. My favourite illustration is the foundation of the Church of England. One of God's creatures called a spirochete got into the brain of Henry VIII, turned him into a megalomaniac, and he founded the Church of England.

CAMERON: That makes the whole process a black comedy, doesn't it? It's also very consonant with my feeling that what underlies your work, and perhaps goes back to the Calvinism of our mutual backgrounds, is really in the last sense a kind of tragic vision of man.

MACLENNAN: That, I think, is perfectly valid of everything I have written so far, except my essays. I think if you are an optimist you are bound to write tragedy; if you are a pessimist you are bound to write comedy. If you are somewhere in between you might produce something like *Measure*

for Measure, or you might even produce *Ulysses*. For the
long term no one could possibly be optimistic, because
whatever has a finite beginning has also a finite end. But even
for the short term you cannot be particularly optimistic
today. Calvin, of course, was dreadful, though the doctrine
of the elect was sort of a barbaric forerunner of Darwinism, I
suppose. But I think I'm at last over Calvinism.

CAMERON: You did say once that you couldn't quarrel
very much with their general sense of the world.

MACLENNAN: This was a while ago. I hope I've grown.
Looking around at the world I've lived in — I've got an enormously long childhood memory and it begins at the end of
1914 — it's not been a wildly encouraging prospect. The old
Presbyterian Sunday-school that I was forced to go to in Nova
Scotia in those days was not as terrifying as a Jesuit seminary
would be in Quebec, but they did their best. I don't believe that
anybody who had ever been forced to memorize the shorter
catechism was ever very comfortable for a long time afterwards. I think my own household was far, far less Calvinistic
in practice than many people were in Nova Scotia in those
days. It's hard to remember what they were like. You might
tell me how old you are.

CAMERON: Thirty-three.

MACLENNAN: Well, you see, I'm sixty-four. Would you
believe that *Two Solitudes* was *savagely* attacked for ob-
scenity when it first came out, *Barometer Rising* even more so,
that you couldn't get a legal drink of anything but beer in what
was then called a beverage parlour, generally a filthy place, in
Toronto until 1951 or '52 when it was known as Drew's Booze
because he put it across? Did you know that Gwethalyn
Graham received letters from all over the country because she
had a young man just about to go overseas spend a weekend
with a girl who was nominally from Westmount? Actually
this should have been Toronto, because the Westmount people
wouldn't have cared. She showed me a letter that said, "This
would be perfectly all right if these characters were American,

but you've made them Canadian. It's untrue and a national insult." I got three letters just before the Halifax VE Day riots, the *very day* before—how could I possible disgrace my people? what would my father's shade be saying?—because I had had this girl have a child out of wedlock just before her fiancé went overseas. And the *next day* the Halifax riot, with a stark-naked Wren directing traffic in front of the Catholic cathedral down there on Spring Garden Road and Barrington Street, and men queued up in relays to get girls into the beds in the furniture stores. This was such a *massive* hypocrisy on the part of the Canadian Calvinists. It was almost unnatural to have to write in those days in Canada. Even the *McGill Alumni News* attacked *Two Solitudes* for being an obscene book. A full professior wrote that editorial, and the Montreal *Gazette* reprinted it. *Barometer Rising* was banned in the public school system of Manitoba in an expurgated and bowdlerized edition in *1962*!

CAMERON: There's been a massive, world wide change ever since 1962.

MACLENNAN: Yes, I don't believe there has been a time where there has ever been such a very large repudiation of what the young and I myself call "the system". Establishment is a lousy word, because it doesn't mean anything. It used to mean something, but "the system"—we know what that is. I think the generation to which I belong turned out ironically to be one of the supreme betraying generations, and therefore to some extent their fate has been tragic, because they were not cynical. They thought they were revolutionaries in the 1930s and they actually thought that socialism was a revolution. Well, of course, it *isn't*. The only revolutions that matter are psychic, somewhere in the human soul, but they believed in political and economic planning, and when they got their hands on the levers of power they were over-confident. As soon as they got into power they replaced a certain amount of high-riding tycoonery with a bureaucracy and what did we get? All you have to do is look at a modern university administration to see what we got.

CAMERON: The reason I was smiling so broadly is that when I went off to Berkeley, people said, Hey, who are the Canadian writers? and I hadn't the faintest idea. You had a similar experience at Oxford, I gather—

MACLENNAN: Oh, nobody asked who a Canadian writer was at any time, when I was young. I resented being called one: I thought I was a writer writing out of Canada.

CAMERON: —but you discovered that young Englishmen there knew more about Canada than you did, had travelled more in Canada—

MACLENNAN: Coming from Nova Scotia I found some did, because—this is on the whole rather healthy—when I was young, people in Cape Breton even talked about going to Nova Scotia. It's reasonable, because it had had a separate history for over a century. We talked about "the New Brunswick frontier". I'd been all over Europe and the States before I got up to Quebec. Nobody knew anything about Canada then but I knew this particular Englishman who had happened to go across the whole country.

CAMERON: In some sense I had to leave Canada to discover—

MACLENNAN: Everybody does, everybody has to leave his own country to see it.

CAMERON: Well, Berkeley gave me this impetus to read some Canadian literature so I'd no longer be embarrassed. I read *The Watch That Ends the Night* and it was a revelation to me because it suggested that there really were whole groups in that generation that really saw the world as it is.

MACLENNAN: This is a little embarrassing to me. I find your reaction very interesting. Professor Raymond Klibanski, who for the past two years has been president of the world philosophic association, was born in Paris and educated in Heidelberg and Oxford. He worked in political warfare in the Hitler war, and he's been a professor at McGill since 1947. He travels much to Europe. He just told me the other day that he had met somebody at Oxford who had read my novel and who said, "It was incredible to me to find that I was deeply involved in all these affairs of the '30s in England where it seemed to be very immediate, but nobody ever touched on it in English fiction after the war was over. This brought the whole thing into a context I had never thought of before." The trouble with Canadian literature is a curious parochialism on the part of people who use the term. I don't think they understand anything of the degree, for example, to which the fiction writers of Canada have been translated all over the world. *The Watch That Ends the Night* went into about six languages; in Germany it sold 250,000 copies in hardback. Farley Mowat claims to have sold 500,000 in Russia but I suppose the Russians pirated him. The Poles wanted to make a television movie out of *Return of the Sphinx. Barometer Rising* is even in Romanian. All told I've been in twelve languages. I suppose Morley Callaghan has been in a great many too. Gwethalyn Graham went into about twelve, with one book only. Yet there is still this feeling that Canadian writers are provincial writers. If I had to live on Canadian sales I'd be absolutely dead, though relatively the market is excellent in Canada, in comparison to the size of the population. On a percentage basis there are many more readers here than in the States. The ordinary public is not a bit self-conscious about reading Canadian writers these days, but the newspaper writers are still nervous about committing themselves. Rob Davies wrote about twelve years ago, when he was writing plays, that a Canadian can't produce a play in Toronto. If he wrote a comedy nobody would laugh at a joke in Toronto unless he had a written guarantee that that same joke had previously been laughed at in London or New York. Nor need we expect the English or the Americans to serve our reputations. The territorial imperative applies to literature, and nobody has ever yielded that willingly to any newcomer. Melville and the early Americans got nowhere in England till after the First World War. French Canadians only broke into France because the Gaullists wished them to. Otherwise, no. A Frenchman before the war asked a friend of mine—and an intelligent Frenchman, an academician—he said, "Are there any English writers except Bernard Shaw?" A famous English writer who shall be nameless invited me to dinner once—I know him quite well, I had him to dinner out here. He had some London critics there, and one of them said, "Look here, don't you think it's about time we started cutting down these South African novelists?" Well, I looked at one of them and said, "'Can you produce over here a novelist in the class of Alan Paton? I think not." He said, "Oh, you can't mean *that!*" "Well," I said, "Of course he's not writing about Mayfair; he's not writing of homosexuals..." I become quite Scotch with them when they get that way.

CAMERON: And the writer who's writing of your own people in your own accent very often can speak to your experience in a way that nobody else could.

MACLENNAN: That's right. The novel is so intimate a form. I used to fret very badly because this country did not offer any characters or fashionable themes and so forth. When I started writing, I really moaned and groaned when I thought Canada was what I was stuck with. I wrote two international novels before I touched Canada, and a publisher said to my agent, "This guy will be a good writer one of these days but we don't know who he is." He didn't know because my New York agent hadn't put my address on the manuscripts. "He's certainly not English," he said, "and he's certainly not American; who is he?" I had a lot of this set in the States and in Europe and so forth. Then it was that I suddenly realized that the novel is such an intimate form that you're stuck with your own country. If the country is not recognizable you have to try to make it so, in order to make your book intelligible. This insight was possibly the origin of such nationalism as I began with, but it matured with the feeling that Canada's success or failure could be no less than make or break for the western world. If we can't make a go of it here, no other new small country is likely to make it. I think that's self-evident.

CAMERON: Peter Buitenhuis comments that your condition forced you to concentrate on content rather than form.

MACLENNAN: That is perfectly true in the earlier work. I concentrated very hard on form in *Two Solitudes* but the book ran away with it and busted it all to pieces, so that I was very unhappy about the form. The form in *Barometer* is artificial. *The Precipice* is something of a chronicle novel, I suppose, so the form is traditional. In the fourth, *Each Man's Son*, I don't think there's anything very much the matter with the form, which is dramatic. But *The Watch That Ends the Night* has a very subtle form. I say that because no critic has ever observed one or two things about it which are supposed to be very difficult to do. For one thing, it's written in the first and third person. Normally, if you start in the first person and you want to get something your narrator can't observe, you get somebody to find a diary where a character will talk about himself privately. But by means of a little bit of timing and shading I found I could jump from the first person directly into the third. I'd never seen it done before like that, but later I discovered a book by Norman Mailer that had been written roughly around the same time, *The Deer Park*, a totally different kind of book. Mailer had done the same thing.

CAMERON: What else about the novel hasn't been picked up by the critics?

MACLENNAN: Oh, the handling of time, of course. The time in the book is a continuum in which the action moves back and forth and up and down. This is something that — forgive me for putting it this way — that one perhaps has to be older to be able to do. Because you're not *aware* of time when you're younger. Time to me now is like an expanding universe. Let's see: when *Barometer* came out I was your age, I was thirty-three. I was still very young —

CAMERON: *Feeling antiquated and exhausted, laughs.*

MACLENNAN: Excuse me for putting it this way, but one year in the life of a man between twenty and twenty-one is equal to about five years between thirty and thirty-five, and could be equal to ten years when you're over forty. Between 35 and 65 time passes in a blur until people suddenly wake up and find they're old. That hasn't happened to me yet, not quite, but all I need is an illness to do it to me. Thus the action in *The Watch* was moving back and forth, I think naturally. The scope of time went all the way back to the '14 war and up to 1952, and I didn't have to work any artificial limits, with statements of dates and so forth, as I did before I understood how to do better with the handling of time. Buitenhuis was dead right about the earlier books. But in any novel, content should be more essential than form. Joyce could let himself go into form and so on because he was writing of one city, and one fundamental situation or problem: the Irish people with their mixed-up nationalism and Catholicism. It's obvious to me that he had bad trouble with form in the *Portrait* but when he got to *Ulysses* he had none at all. It's very easy to handle time in a book where the action takes place in twenty-four hours.

CAMERON: But with *Return of the Sphinx* the criticism is once again a formal criticism, the feeling being that the whole thing is very diffuse, that the centres of consciousness move around in a relatively unrelated way —

MACLENNAN: I don't talk back to critics usually, but now I'm getting so I don't care, because in recent years so many of our critics have become cocksure and ‑arbitrary. It takes a writer to *write* a book, it takes a reader to *read* a book, and a combination of both of them *makes* a book; and maybe some of the critics will accept this one of these days. If *The Sphinx* moved too fast for them, maybe it wasn't entirely my fault. I'll simply say that *The Sphinx* is the best book I ever wrote, formally. There's not a psychological equation that was wrong in that. I was stopped in the bank by a completely strange man, a European psychiatrist, who said he had read *The Sphinx* five times over. "I don't know how it is that artists are ahead of reality," he said. "I'm loaded up with patients that come right out of your novel right now." So the critics thought it was diffuse. It's exactly the opposite. I was saying in a sentence what previously I would have taken a paragraph for. Now I'm writing a new book, and the concision I used in *The Sphinx* will probably be absent from it. Concision is not appropriate to an age as diffuse as ours. Now I find I'm writing a very tempestuous prose compared to what I wrote in the past.

CAMERON: Really? In that short a time?

MACLENNAN: That's right. That's because I have three hundred students here and I'm living in a revolutionary province. If you look at music, it's the best analogy. I'm not — please, because I mention Beethoven we're not making any comparisons, you know! But the situation could apply to even pygmies. You must reflect the movement of your times. Otherwise you die if you're an artist of any sort. Now, Beethoven's "Eroica", the Third Symphony, was finished in 1804 and ten years later Beethoven wrote the Seventh Symphony, which had its première at the Congress of Vienna. The Seventh is a new kind of music that nobody'd ever heard before. It's *violent*, it's *staccato*, it's *jerky*, it's *boisterous*, it's *explosive*! It's because Beethoven was in touch with the violence of Napoleon's time. Then he went into retreat, and he came back with those tremendous contemplative things of his last period.

CAMERON: You say it's a revolutionary province. Do you expect a revolution?

MACLENNAN: We may be two-thirds over it. The Catholic religion here was so tight in 1960 that the word divorce couldn't be mentioned on the screen of a Quebec theatre, and a married woman couldn't be shown being kissed. At the moment I think there are twenty-one pornographic films, and half of them made in Quebec, showing in Montreal. I don't say this is good, but I say it's a fact. The French-Canadian birth-rate used to be the highest in the western hemisphere; now it may be one of the lowest. The sexual revolution hit Quebec simultaneously with the explosion of the religion, followed by *la politique de grandeur*, which came out of the sudden eruption of a new middle class. Marx was in my opinion dead right when he said the middle class is revolution-

ary. The proletariat is never revolutionary. It's the most conservative—I know it is. I grew up in a mining town. Just look
at working men. Most of them would love to get rid of their
union leaders right now. But the bourgeoisie will always make
a revolution. All that gang that made the revolution in Russia
were bourgeois. They got the proletariat with them, so they
said. The hell they got the proletariat with them, they got the
starving *army* with them!

CAMERON: It's that close for you, that is, that change in the
period of five years—

MACLENNAN: Look, there has been many a day in the lives of
any of us who are sensitive people living in this city, French
or English, when we didn't know when we got up in the
morning what we'd be thinking when we went to bed at night.

CAMERON: You're very sensitive to the interaction of public
events and private events and the way that each affects the
other.

MACLENNAN: Well, they always do. Jane Austen managed to
avoid the tempests of her time, but then she was in a very
unique social position. Joyce, I suppose, was about as ego-
centric a writer as ever lived, and his egotism was sufficiently
enormous that he ignored contemporary events like the 1914
war. But only a few weeks ago I picked up a sentence of D.H.
Lawrence, who said the novel begins at the point where the
soul encounters history. Of all people to say that, Lawrence
would have been the last I would have thought of, but I think
what he says is true. How can any writer in the twentieth
century avoid history? Most of us would like to, but I don't see
how it's possible. Joyce, after all, was a late Victorian in his
personal life.

CAMERON: Then is your work historical fiction set in the
present? Historical fiction in the kind of sense that Lukács
talks about?

MACLENNAN: It's hard for me to answer that, but I think if I
understand your question I'd have to say yes. I did have a
historical training, as you probably know, though it was in

ancient history. The most modern subject anybody could study today would be the Roman Empire, particularly if you. get into its taxation system. It's made the task of writing more complicated for me than for most writers, because I tear up more than anybody I know. I'm apt to be too discursive in the original drafts, one idea leading to another, till I've put too much stuff in, and then perhaps I pare too much out, I don't know. I'm trying to evolve a style now where I can get it all in naturally, as Rebecca West does, in her own particular way, when she's really opening up the taps. Yet I think that we in the twentieth century are certainly the most self-consciously historical civilization there's ever been. But God, history in the twentieth century —

CAMERON: My guess is that you'd have more respect for Freud than Marx, all the same.

MACLENNAN: My position to Freud is very respectful — it isn't of Marx, not really. Marx interested me mainly because he surely got most of his historical stuff from the Roman Empire. Marx is a very good guide for a lot of that. I was nearly kicked out of Princeton on account of my thesis because they thought I was a Marxist. But the tragedy of Freud has not been exposed. He took the biology that was given him by contemporary biologists and much of this was inaccurate and may have led him to his over-emphasis of sex. Sex is not the main cause of aggression.

CAMERON: What *is* the cause of aggression?

MACLENNAN: Genetic inheritance, mostly. That has been proved pretty well by now. When the scientists found out that man developed from the weapon-carrying ape, the source of aggression was clear. Why the hell do people like to play tennis and above all, why do they feel good afterwards? The tennis racket is just about the length of an antelope bone.

CAMERON: From an old tennis player this is an interesting comment!

MACLENNAN: I used to feel pure as a lamb after five sets of tennis. There's some element of aggression in sex, but that element isn't the cause of war. Robert Ardrey is unanswerable when he says, How many people have died of love or sex in the twentieth century, compared to how many people have died for property? Freud was wrong in the matter of sex to a large extent, I think. I accept, generally speaking, his breakdown of the human personality, and his discovery of the subconscious. But the Oedipus complex to me is fundamentally not sexual: it's a fight for authority. I don't believe it is a struggle fundamentally to get into bed with your mother.

CAMERON: A question of power.

MACLENNAN: I would say so, yes.

CAMERON: You're very conscious of differences, say, between generations.

MACLENNAN: When you reach a certain time in your life, and you're about the right age now, for the next ten years everything is expanding for you. Exciting and wonderful and all fresh. But later you see these repetitions, and you get the sense of *déjà vu*, and you feel the poignancy of cross generations and perhaps you find yourself in a position that I personally do, of having had to make terms with a generation that I've never really got along with. I've many friends among it, but I've never been able to be myself in it and I've had to live in disguise almost like Robin Hood to survive in it. I've been more at home with people of student years, and I think it's fair to say they seem to be equally so with me. I work very hard with them. That's why I come here, to meet them, those who are, say, anywhere between eighteen and twenty-three or twenty-four. Sometimes this association adds a very great poignancy, because I would have *liked* to have belonged to their generation. There's a remarkable generosity and naturalness in them. Hypocrisy exists only among the left-wing politically oriented ones, who are not hypocritical, really. Most of the ones I knew here were cynical.

CAMERON: And there are young people in both your most recent novels. I noticed in *Return of the Sphinx* you have a transcript of a TV interview with Aimé La Tendresse, and a

passage from Hansard, and so on. It reminded me of Jerry
Rubin's *DO IT!* and, oddly, of Sterne, this visual thing.

MACLENNAN: Well, I'm not a conscious experimenter; I'm
just doing what I have to do to get the book to move. Now anybody knows today that literature's problem is to survive
television. It's not going to be easy, though I expect literature
can survive anything. But television! Can society survive it?
It puts the greatest moral responsibility on an *animateur* and
very few of them assume that responsibility. Television is
absolutely unreal. Nobody ever remembers anything clearly
and in sequence that they see on it. McLuhan is for the birds
as far as I'm concerned and yet he's right in a certain way when
he says the TV medium is the real message here. That is, no
real message. It's McLuhan's opportunism that annoys me and
his appalling use of the English language. However, if you
want to reach the public you must get on TV. If you want to
sell a book now, you must get on TV. It used to be radio, which
was clearer. People *listen* on radio, but nobody's going to
listen to a book being read on television. It's visual, and it's *got*
to be visual. Now there have been very sensational television
shows, politically. The French network was loaded down
with separatists for a while. You could get a man looking
straight in the eye of the audience—I've *heard* them, for God's
sake—"Yes, bombs and shootings in the streets." They didn't
say it before I had written it though, but I knew they were
going to say it sooner or later.

CAMERON: Does this produce the need to get something
visual in the novel?

MACLENNAN: I always try to get things visual in a novel, but
if I were starting a revolution, I'd try to get on television. It's
perfect for the revolutionary, especially when everybody
was favouring youth. *La Jeunesse Parle.* Some of the young
TV hands are damn good. My God, I've heard students interviewed on some of these shows who are far better than I could
ever dream of being on that medium. They seem to take to it
naturally, perhaps because they grew up with it and know

exactly how to handle it. My use of the Hansard thing in the novel was something else again. Canada went through a series of debates of extreme violence when the Dief was on the loose in the House, and if a fictional character was in Parliament, as my Alan Ainslie was, Hansard would be the source for what he said and for what his enemies said against him. That's why I used the Hansard device in *The Sphinx*.

CAMERON: We've talked a bit about fathers and sons, but not about justice. Isn't that one of your obsessions?

MACLENNAN: I think it is the basis of practically all important literary art. It's at the bottom of every play Euripides wrote. It's at the bottom of everything that Sophocles and Aeschylus wrote. It's at the bottom of practically everything Shakespeare wrote. If you ask me that question—I'm damn glad you did—I'd like to close off with this: if you want to read a novel, and it happens to have been written by a Canadian, which I think has poignantly, marvellously, and succinctly concentrated the whole dilemma of justice in an organized society, it's Colin McDougall's *Execution*.

May 3, 1971

Hugh MacLennan:
Biography and Bibliography

Born in Glace Bay, Nova Scotia, in 1907, Hugh MacLennan grew up in Halifax, adding a Rhodes Scholarship to a Dalhousie B.A. He subsequently won a Ph.D. at Princeton, specializing in Roman history, and, in the absence of university jobs during the Depression, began teaching at Lower Canada College in Montreal in 1935, a job he held for ten years. From 1945 to 1951 he lived as a free-lance writer and broadcaster, but since 1951 he has taught English at McGill. His first wife, Dorothy Duncan, also a writer, died some years ago. MacLennan has remarried, and now lives in an old brick apartment building off Côte des Neiges Road in the winter, and at North Hatley, in the Eastern Townships, during the summer. He has won a Guggenheim Fellowship, a Fellowship in the Royal Society of Canada, and five Governor General's Awards.

Fiction

Barometer Rising (1941)
Two Solitudes (1945)
The Precipice (1948)
Each Man's Son (1951)
The Watch that Ends the Night (1959)
Return of the Sphinx (1967)

Essays

Cross Country (1949)
Thirty and Three (1954)
Scotchman's Return and Other Essays (1960)

Other Works

Oxyrhynchus (Ph.D. dissertation, published 1968)
Seven Rivers of Canada (1961)
The Colour of Canada (1967)

Criticism

Peter Buitenhuis, Hugh MacLennan (1969)
Robert Cockburn, The Novels of Hugh MacLennan (1969)
Alec Lucas, Hugh MacLennan (1970)
George Woodcock, Hugh MacLennan (1969)
See also Edmund Wilson, O Canada: An American's Notes on
     Canadian Culture (1965)

David Lewis Stein :

Journalism, Politics, and Pornography

Battered suede hat balanced on the back of his head, a tooth-pick thrusting from his mouth, steel-rimmed glasses glinting in the neon lights, David Lewis Stein stumps up Yonge Street at three in the morning, revelling in the fecundity and garish-

ness of this most crass of main stems. Stein has worked for the New York Herald-Tribune *in Paris, lived in New York, travelled with the Yippies in Chicago; nevertheless he is steeped in Toronto. When he entered the Sai Woo Restaurant at midnight, the waiter said, "Hi, Dave, shall I order for you?" for Stein is an habitué who has frequented the Sai Woo now for fifteen years, since he was an undergraduate at the University of Toronto.*

From Defoe to Orwell and Hemingway, journalism and politics have bred many a novelist — but, oddly, not often in Canada. As a novelist who earns his living reporting on municipal politics, Stein lives at that historic crossroads, almost alone among Canadian novelists in finding his subject in the politics of his own time.

Earlier in the evening, in his office in the almost-deserted Toronto Star building on King Street, Stein had thrown his chunky little frame back in his chair, balanced a microphone on his lap, and muttered darkly about Toronto and its politics, about public and private life, about politics and fiction. A man of the left, he had passionately denounced the extremes of the left, and worried about the uncertain possibility of bearing human witness through the arts of fiction.

CAMERON: What do you do at the *Star*?
STEIN: I started out here as kind of an artsy-craftsy columnist, doing this column called *The City*. I was slowly but surely drawn more and more into municipal politics because after all city hall was always a good source of things going on. Then last fall they put me in charge of municipal editorial writing. I ran away with that and since last fall I've become a kind of guerilla editorial writer or something. It got me into this whole conflict between being a private person and a totally political person. I wrote a column last week that made everybody mad at me, like virtually *everybody*. It was very funny: I had one

of the leading super citizens and a developer both call me up
to bawl me out for the same column. I was looking at it in a
kind of literary way, I was seeing it as a drama and finding
that my side has pretty awful people in some ways, with the
terrible smugness and sanctimoniousness of the reformer, and
that they all operate on the devil theory: all we've got to do
is get rid of those evil men, and *we*, the forces of goodness,
truth, and beauty, will take over, and the world will be fine.
They don't concede, or can't understand, that these guys are
simply responses to problems that are going to exist whether
they're there or not. They say this council's in the pocket of
developers and one way or another that's probably true. But
the developers are responding to problems: the developers
don't operate in a vacuum and neither do the politicians. And
I was seeing this in a very literary, dramatic way, and wrote the
column that way. Of course I infuriated everybody, because
you've got to be partisan, and you have to choose your side.
You can't be a literary man any more. But I accept this, I
realize the necessity for this now.

CAMERON: In fiction as well?

STEIN: Well, my new novel is very political. But I don't make
a distinction. I'm a writer: I put as much energy and imagination into writing an editorial as I do into writing a short story.
You're not supposed to do those things, but I do. When I first
started ten years ago the best writing in this country was journalism, not fiction. The academic bias, the academic stupidity,
militated against really understanding what the journalists
were doing. I was at *Maclean's* in those really good years
when Lefolii and Gzowski were running it; Barb Moon was
there, and Sidney Katz, and funny old McKenzie Porter. The
people that they were able to tap as free-lancers were
amazing. In a sense, a nationalistic sense of Canada really
came out of what was created by journalists.

CAMERON: You do presumably draw *some* distinction between journalism and fiction. What is it?

STEIN: Well, the obvious, working out of one's imagination.

But if you have the kind of leeway I have around here, you apply a lot of imagination and analysis to what you're doing too, to the facts. In fact I often use the facts to write fiction, which gets me into trouble. There are the obvious facile distinctions that one can make, but if you're approaching it as a writer, I find the distinctions much more difficult. I suppose I'm a better journalist than I am a novelist, and I like journalism.

CAMERON: The kind of fiction you've done has a lot of connections with journalism too. Like *Scratch One Dreamer*.

STEIN: Sure, the genesis of that — part of it anyway, the demonstration — was a demonstration I was sent to cover in Quebec in La Macaza. Part of the understanding of the town was another place I was sent as a journalist, up in Sudbury. A lot of the stories I couldn't tell as a journalist, I just put in the novel. I was up there when Mine Mill was being raided by Steel. I came close to getting clobbered a couple of times, but I managed to establish that I was neutral, so I could go between these two hostile camps. Guys were getting creamed in alleys and things like that; it was a very vicious fight and they accepted me, you know — funny little journalist from Toronto. So I'd go out drinking every night with a different crew, and I got right into the heart of it. Guys started spilling out the whole Communist connection and I knew a lot of the old Commies down here, partly from another story I'd done for *Maclean's*. That was the beautiful part of being a magazine writer. When we all walked out of *Maclean's* it was like losing one's innocence.

CAMERON: But you enjoy writing fiction?

STEIN: Yeah, I really enjoyed writing this novel; nobody else is going to like it, but I like it, and that satisfies me. I've had trouble getting it published. I've faced the fact that I've probably spent a couple of years on something that I wasn't going to get published, and that's pretty cold stuff to take. And the feeling you get is, Has it been a total waste of time? But what I began to feel was, I don't give a damn, I really enjoyed doing this, it was really a pleasure. I was by myself, I had no one to answer to or explain anything to. I could live totally inside my own imagination. It was totally mine. But it's like a hobby now, you can't be a serious novelist. And also the demands that are made on your time and energy as a journalist, are such that you become more and more involved in the political fight. It becomes increasingly difficult to know what you are, where you fit as an artist. In any case, who gives a damn in this country? It's great to be a novelist when nobody reads novels and there's hardly anybody left to publish them.

CAMERON: But you go on doing it.

STEIN: Yes, I think this is a good novel, despite what everybody else is going to say about it, and I live in hope that somebody's going to buy it for the movies and I can live on the interest for the rest of my life or something like that. But, being practical about it, or cold-blooded about it, it's very discouraging to be a writer. I grew up in the '50s, in which to be an artist was a big deal, particularly for middle-class kids, because it meant you were rejecting your parents—these dull, crass, middle-class people. It was as close as we got to any form of rebellion from the traditions that we were put into. And you somehow imagined that this was going to be enough, this would justify your existence, the world would applaud you and support you. But none of this is true. We function in a very political time.

CAMERON: Tell me about this novel. What's it called? and why don't people like it?

STEIN: It's called *My Sexual and Other Revolutions*, which probably tells you enough right there. It's pornographic and political. It's a very serious novel—nobody's going to believe that—but it's a very serious novel, although it's intended to be funny and parts of it are. But it's a tract about violence and non-violence, an attempt to deal with some of the problems, people spouting revolutionary ideology. I don't buy a double theory of history any more. I suppose the kidnappings and the murder in October were a crisis of conscience for me. Would you like to live in a society run by the Rose brothers?

That's a question you've got to ask. Christ, the Rose brothers would kill anybody or anything, and justify it. You've got to put your own life on the line if you're going to become a revolutionary. Well, I'm not prepared to put my life on the line to put people like Rose and Lortie and that whole sad little crew in power. I'm tired of people who want to go out and kill for peace, which is the kind of total insanity you get with these guys to pull off a kidnapping. There's something particularly ugly about the way they killed Laporte, something so inhuman and stupid about it. I'm tired of children playing at changing society. There's a kind of bad coinage in politics, it's a game of chicken: I'm prepared to murder people for the revolution, why aren't you? You, you fat middle-class bourgeois revisionist slob, I'm going to *die*, I'm actually going to *kill* somebody, I'm going to blow something up. That means that you've got to blow something up or you're not a revolutionary any more. You get these meaningless phrases, like Power to the People — fat little girl sociology students on their way to Europe for the summer shouting "*Power to the People!*" Stupid.

CAMERON: It sounds as though you've abandoned any kind of revolutionary view, but I don't think that's what you're saying.

STEIN: No, no. I suppose if anything in a sense I'm more radical, but I'm very opposed to violence now. I've seen a little of mob violence myself, I've been part of mobs. I had a moment of truth about that too. It was November of '69 and I went to the demonstration at the Justice Department, this big, supposedly non-violent thing. Don't ever believe that, when they tell you it's non-violent. When you're in a crowd of 250,000 you don't feel peaceful at all. There's a sense of menace, of the power of a mob, and the violence is *right there*.

CAMERON: Robin Mathews calls himself a red tory. Are you becoming one, too?

STEIN: Probably. I support most of Mathews; I certainly agree with all the good fights he's waged at the universities. I think of myself more as a kind of anarchist in the sense that I really distrust anything that's institutionalized and organized. I recognize the necessity for all of these things, but I've come to distrust all of them. I distrust movements, I distrust anybody who has answers, I suppose. It's a terrible position to be in. It gets back in a sense to the conflict which politics forces you into, of becoming this kind of public figure. I want my privacy, I want my private mind, I want my right to dissent from the truth.

CAMERON: — to go to hell in your own way?

STEIN: Yeah. I don't want to lead my life as a totally political life, and yet I'm beginning to feel there's just no alternative. We're going to work towards the new forms we need in the way we lead our own lives. A politics in which you go out of your house, you do your little political thing, and you go back to your house and close the door, that doesn't work any more. I wish it did. It's a much more comfortable way of life, particularly if you want to write novels.

CAMERON: So do we surrender such things as the luxury of private life, the luxury of writing a novel as an art form rather than a political document? Or do we find a way of making a political document an art form?

STEIN: Well, in that sense, my ideal is Orwell, who was also a journalist. I think one of the things we've got to work for is a level of self-consciousness, knowledge of our own society, which we just don't have. We just really don't know who's running this country. It's really interesting. *New York* magazine did a thing about the ten most powerful people in New York. They had about four or five giving their opinions of who were the most powerful people, and there were some that were on everybody's list like David Rockefeller from the Chase Manhattan, and the publisher of the *Times*. One guy listed a Mafia head as one of the most powerful people, and he told why — it was very interesting: all of these people know a hell of a lot about New York. A few weeks later the *Telegram* did this in Toronto — the ten most powerful people in Toronto.

One of them was the publisher of the *Telegram*. Now he may
be a lot of other things, but he's not one of the most powerful
people in Toronto. In the two people they picked in city hall,
they got one wrong. I sat down and said, Well, who the hell
would I list as the ten most powerful people? I could get up
to about three. I just don't know. I think this is where Mathews
is so right: as long as we get these fucking expatriates up here
we're never going to find out, because they don't care.

CAMERON: What's behind that title, *My Sexual and Other
Revolutions*?

STEIN: Oh, it's a nice title. Quite seriously. Very little to do
with the book.

CAMERON: You didn't really tell me why people dislike it.

STEIN: Not even my wife likes it; she says it's too ugly and
dirty. I'll read you a couple of pages, and that'll tell you why
people don't like it.

CAMERON: Great.

STEIN: In this chapter, the novel is exploring revolutionary
forms, and myths, and language, and it goes through many
forms of revolutionary action, from non-violence to various
forms of violence, though I didn't realize this when I was
writing it. I didn't really know what I was doing as I was
writing it, except enjoying myself.

[At this point Stein read pp. 139-41 of the published novel.
Halfway through it, the secretary noted on the transcript—
DON! THAT'S ENOUGH, I JUST ATE DINNER. SURELY
YOU DON'T NEED THIS CRAP.]

CAMERON: Right, I can see why people dislike it. But look, it's
a very funny parody of a sex scene.

STEIN: Well, I think it's really hilarious. I've had some funny
experiences with it. I sent it out to Gonick, to try to get it into
Dimension, and he said, Well, we'd like to do it, but we're
worried about the reaction from Women's Lib. And he was
serious! You really get great reactions with this stuff.

CAMERON: A lot of the younger novelists are working with
fantasy, with forms that are not realistic in the old sense at all.
And with humour, too.

STEIN: That's interesting. In my case it's a response to the fact that, as a journalist, to go home and write a realistic novel is too much like work. Also I think that, for me anyway, it's just the only response. I won't do this again; what I want to do next is something quite different—fantasy but different.

CAMERON: Has the whole world become so totally insane that all that's left to do is to laugh about it?

STEIN: No, I wouldn't say that. I think it's a kind of protest fiction. If you do protest fiction like I did initially, about people and demonstrations, it gets pretty boring. You protest in fiction by satirizing the society that you're in, so in a sense it's a very political fiction. It's a kind of shorthand way to re-create the society. If you're doing it realistically you have to do it in the way that people live, in a sense, and you discover things only dimly. And that's what I really want to write about, the evolution of people's consciousness. When you're doing it in fantasy you're able to bring together things from the society. It's a mirror image of the society anyway; it's not totally fantastic. It's a perception of the society we live in, and you're able to bring things closer. By juxtaposing them you show the inconsistencies of it. You can expose more easily what's wrong with it in fantasy than you can by trying to be realistic. I don't think of it as fantasy in the sense the Wizard of Oz is fantasy.

CAMERON: —but in the way that Kafka is fantasy?

STEIN: Yes, 'exactly.

CAMERON: So then humour is also part of the attack?

STEIN: Most definitely, sure. It's also part of the entertainment. It's a lot of work to read a novel, so you want to make it as entertaining as you can. It's also fun, you know? Shit, I want to *enjoy* it. I really enjoyed writing this. You get a hard-on writing all these sex things. I had fun, which I haven't had in writing for a long time.

CAMERON: Maybe the human response to the horrible state of the world is to kind of acknowledge it but dance on it. There's a sense of almost defiant play.

STEIN: Well, I would say more that the response is, you reduce it to manageable proportions, like Dr. Strangelove. You reduce nuclear death to a joke because there's no other way; you just can't live with the reality if you let it sink into you. I think you would go mad. We live in a mad, insane society. This kind of writing relieves the tension of the writer and it also allows him to kind of deal with the enormity of it, by making it unreal.

CAMERON: When private life has become part of a political enormity, do novelists perforce give us political fiction?

STEIN: Yes, but — What are the models for political novels? Camus? Orwell? I think Orwell's almost more important for the journalism than he is for the novels he wrote at the end of his life. If you read his collected journalism, the evolution of a political mind is just amazing. He's my great hero in a sense, because he's so ordinary. He gives me hope for myself. He starts off as a very ordinary man, *very* ordinary man, and he never loses that quality of being an ordinary man. He has no illusions about himself as a writer. Read his letters to his publishers and critics: no pretensions to art at all. His novels were intended to be political, and his minor novels are much more important to read. Do you know *Keep the Aspidistra Flying*? It's a masterpiece, just a marvellous insight to the commercial society. Even *The Clergyman's Daughter* is a fantastic novel. *Coming Up for Air* is just incredible. I'm really impressed by this ordinariness, although I want to lead an intellectual life. I make no apologies for being an intellectual, I consider myself an intellectual. I want to be an ordinary man and an intellectual. And a novelist. In our day, that's a tall order.

June 26, 1971

David Lewis Stein:
Biography and Bibliography

Born in 1937, raised and educated in Toronto, David Lewis Stein has been a journalist with Canadian Press, Maclean's *magazine (1960-4), the Paris edition of the New York* Herald Tribune *(1965-7), and the* Toronto Daily Star *(1969-71). In 1964-5, a Canada Council grant enabled him to write his first novel, in London; during 1967-9 he worked in New York as a free lance writer under contract to the* Star Weekly, *an arrangement which enabled him to travel for some time with the Yippies. He now lives in Toronto with his wife and two children, studying urban planning at the University of Toronto under a Southam Fellowship.*

Fiction

Scratch One Dreamer (1967)
New Canadian Writing 1968 (with Clark Blaise and Dave Godfrey)
My Sexual and Other Revolutions (1971)

Non-Fiction

Living the Revolution: The Yippies in Chicago (1969)